MEDICINE WORDS FOR YOUR
BRAVE REVOLUTION

FREEDOM

MEDICINE WORDS FOR YOUR
BRAVE REVOLUTION

Soul Water Rising

Camarillo, California

Printed in the United States of America

Soul Water Rising
Camarillo, California
soulwater.org

Library of Congress Control Number: 2020906564
ISBN 978-0-9987802-2-1

First Soul Water Rising Edition, Softcover: 2020

Inspiration / Social Issues

Editors: Jacqueline V. Carter
           Kent W. Mortensen

Cover & Interior Design: Jaiya John

These words are dedicated to you.

For what you give for us.

For what it takes from you.

We have studied the mountains and their tenure.
They tell us you cannot break the sky.
If you stay sky, you stay free.

We have pondered the sequoia and their reign.
They tell us if you are rooted,
you can stand through all things.

We have witnessed the rivers and their range.
They tell us all borders are illusion.
Spirit shapes this mystic world.

ORIGIN STORY:

A TALE OF THE SUPREMACY-INFERIORITY VIRUS

The ancient ones tell of a legend.

In the beginning, two spirits roamed every soul. One was Love. The other, fear. Fear, being restless and unsettled, mutated into two other spirits: supremacy and inferiority. Both of these would inhabit every human soul and space, forever. Waiting. To be fed.

This is the Love story of our freedom from supremacy and inferiority. Freedom from oppression. Our freedom to live a beautiful life.

•

Supremacy and inferiority are identical twins posing as opposites. They were conceived in the same womb of fear. Suckled from the same breast and of the same milk. Walk now in the same world. Are sustained by the same atmosphere of fear. Touch one and you touch the other. Mend one and you purify the other. Learn how they live and die together. Be a student of their ways. If you know them, you can find them. Where you find them, you can heal their hollow hum.

Supremacy, born from fear's womb, is actually a sense of inferiority. An existential insecurity. You can only feel this way if you have lost, or never truly had an active, living

7

relationship with the natural world. Only if you exist as a disconnected, ravenous creature with a dire need to consume, conquer, and control. Those overcome with supremacy sickness do not actually feel supreme. They feel terrified and weak. In their mind, they truly believe they are supreme. This belief does not reach down to their soul, the place that determines their ability to exist in harmony with the world. Their soul taunts them. Tells them through spirit that no matter what they believe, in their supremacy condition they are somehow fatally flawed. Insufficient. Their unfortunate remedy for this feeling? To grow consumed with further fabricating a belief that they are supreme.

Supremacy says to itself, *I am supreme. My kind are supreme. We belong at the center of the world. If we are not at the center, on top, in front, first, and in control, the world will fall apart. We are innately superior and qualified. The others are innately inferior and unqualified. If we let them through our doors, we will sacrifice quality. I need to wrap myself in a security blanket of my kind. What my kind thinks, feels, says, produces, creates is superior. My kind has the right to go anywhere in the world and make it in our image. Everyone will be better off then, because we are supreme. God made us supreme. We are following natural order by upholding our supremacy. We will change laws and outward customs to keep the others docile, but we will not change our hearts. We will always believe our way is the best way. We will create tests in our image that prove our superior intelligence. We will build systems in our image that appear to serve lives but that exist to control lives, to preserve our supremacy. We must locate ourselves at the center of every story. We must be the savior of every story. We will take the saviors and prophets of every story and cast them in our image. Daily we must affirm in every mind our supremacy. Anyone and anything that challenges our supremacy must be destroyed.*

Inferiority says to itself, *I am inferior. My kind are inferior. We will talk bravely about being beautiful and capable, but in our private soul, we feel our inferiority. We must appease the superior ones. The central dictate of our lives is to keep the superior ones comfortable with us. With our presence. With our existence. We cannot manage in this world without them. They know better, do better, are better. The entire world will fall apart if we inferior ones are in front, on top, at the center, first, or in control. We are terrified of building and creating our own lives, our own systems and societies. We do not believe in ourselves. If any of us dares to challenge the superior ones or their supremacy, we will destroy that one, that one who threatens to ruin our comfortable reality. We suffer oppression, but that is our fate, it is who we are. We run from our heritage, our history, our ancestors, our traditions and customs and rituals and ways. We run from our language and values. We run from our own natural bodies, hair, and expression. We run from abundance and joy, from Love and kindness, from anything soft and nurturing. We belong to hard days and hard ways. We will live in this pain forever.*

A virus will transform its host into a condition and environment that best suits the virus. An atmosphere in which the virus can flourish. A gut virus will change the acidity of the gut to a level prime for the multiplication of the virus. An oppression virus will change the cellular nature of its host to defend and foster that virus. The very spirit of the host will change. Defensiveness, fragility. Inability to deal with discomfort, shame, or guilt. Violence, anger, rage. Inability to relate to oppressed people as reciprocal human beings. A need for dominance, control, social power. All of these internal conditions protect and feed the virus, perpetuating the generational epidemic.

When a mind is colonized by a poisonous idea, it rearranges its structures and chemistry to be a good host for that idea. The mind becomes the womb, nest, and protective fortress for that idea. The mind does not discern good idea from bad idea. It only wants to be a good host for any idea a person chooses to activate. Supremacy-inferiority virus sets up its central colony in the mind. Revolution sparks and lives and dies in the mind. Healing gathers its forces in the mind. The mind then, is the creator of our emotional, behavioral ways of being. When unwell, these ways serve to reinforce the processing of the colonized mind. A colonized mind is a hive mind, protected by collective ways deepened through generational transmission.

Repetition of an idea is how an idea crystallizes in this world. Then spreads on the winds of social repetition. Repetition of ideas is how you oppress a people. It is how you create social order and hierarchy. Repetition is how you sicken souls and lives and make putrid a nation. Repetition is also the ceremony and ritual for healing all that has been dehumanized. The way into the plague is also the way out: Repetition. Of humanizing, sacred ideas. Repetition of communal emotions and behaviors. Repetition of sowing, harvesting, and feasting on communal rewards. Don't be afraid to repeat yourself.

Colonization is the act of transforming an ecosystem into a climate that fosters the survival and dominance of an invasive spirit and kind. It has nothing to do with benevolence or sharing resources. Colonization isn't an improvement project. It is a murderous rampage. It cannot succeed without death of the preexisting native occupants. It changes the energetic composition of an environment from harmonious to toxic, so the colonizer may then thrive in that toxicity. What then does this say about the nature and composition of the colonizer? We need to answer this question, and make widely known the answer.

Supremacy virus calcifies the pineal gland, deadening people's spiritual conduction of Love. This creates a power outage. People lose sight. Of Sacredness. They become incapable of seeing those they deem inferior. The supposed inferior ones become an invisible class. Soulfully blind, supremacy-sickened souls stumble around the world bruising and damaging everything. Including themselves and the ones they Love.

The tendency to arrange humans in hierarchy, caste, order, class, rank, title, and status is not human nature. It is a human condition. A condition that arises as souls drift from their spirit root, and fear and insecurity arise. Human nature is freedom. Aspiring toward royalty is not liberation. It is further subjugation. Of those crowned. And those downed by the demeaning of crownless masses. Dispense with crowns and thrones and castles. Disrobe your identity and pride, walk naked out into the common field, and learn to be with the people in sacred ways. This is our freedom challenge.

Viral contagions in the form of human groups want you to believe they are superior. That it is inevitable you will live infected and rendered in their image. They will never stop whispering, *Create optimal conditions for us and you too can be a favored one. You can live a superior life.*

Supremacy is the most malicious terrorism.
It is state-sponsored, ever present, daily assault.

Supremacy spirits believe they rule the world. Truly, they are ruled by their supremacy obsession. They are overseers whose shift never ends. They wield the whip so endlessly, it becomes an appendage they cannot bear to sever. Blisters form not on their palms, but in their hearts. Hearts which then suffer not being able to perform their native Love.

Signs you have been infected (if not overrun) with the supremacy virus: You have a persistent urge to be at the center of everything. You believe yourself to be the ultimate authority on other peoples' lives. You feel anxious with unfavored groups having any control. Over their lives. Over yours. Your back suddenly stiffens when the situation calls for you to bow in humility to another living thing. Nothing has been discovered until your kind discovers it. Nothing is valid until your kind validates it. Nothing is valuable until your kind values it. You feel the need to recast everything in your image. You expect unfavored people to protect your feelings and comfort even as your attitudes and actions and silence and complicity harm their lives. All stories must glorify you. You expect everyone to speak in your language. You don't feel safe unless surrounded by your kind. You resent your kind when they show Love and honor to the unfavored kind. Your soul and spirit are strangled inside you daily, strangled by your fear of other people's presence and freedom. You have a hard time releasing tension from your body due to lifelong suppression of guilt and shame, so you walk the world a stiff, robotic thing, resentful of anyone who makes you feel. You stay inside your intellect, which protects you from feelings of absolute pain for participating in generational oppression. You dream of joining the rest of humanity even as you resent and treat them like something to wash off of the pristine essence you believe yourself to be. You live like the victim of childhood fairytales. Tales that said you and your kind were the Beauty, and the unfavored kind were the Beast. You live like you believe in those lies. Your soul and aura are bent over from the weight of maintaining those lies every breath of your life. You desperately want a place to land, but being on the humble ground without artificial elevation terrifies you, so you go on, an exhausted, empty thing caught in a lonely wind.

Supremacy virus Loves to travel underground. Under laws and policies. Under propaganda and rhetoric. Under false cultural narratives. Under ignorance and miseducation. Under denial and avoidance. Under token reparative efforts. All of these insulate supremacy virus, allowing it to never be scorched by the sunlight of public and personal revelation and reckoning. If you take a virus out from its cool, wet place beneath a rotting log and place it on the open baking face of a boulder beneath the sun, the virus will not long survive. This is how you kill supremacy.

Supremacy is an insecure spirit. It perceives constant assault on its lie. It was pathological to begin with, or it wouldn't have manifested as supremacy. Supremacy is counter to the nature of nature. Supremacy is so insecure, it is compelled to cast gods in its image. To erect monuments to its glory. Rename landmarks to idealize its heroes. Supremacy is a paranoia and narcissism that makes for an anxious, terrified world.

Supremacy spirit and conquest spirit both concentrate in particular cultures according to those cultures' ways of being. Cultural roots ingrained in conflict attract and foster such spirits. Communal, spiritual, earth culture roots act as a repellent against infection from supremacy and conquest virus. Spirit humbles people and creates communion. The abandonment of Spirit does the opposite.

Supremacy creates a crisis of confidence in everyone at the idea of the labeled inferior ones being in control of anything. Few will admit publicly to the absence of belief in the competence of the inferior ones. Most will be soaked in this disbelief. Such that they hold faith in supposed superior ones even if they are clowns. If clowns are in control long enough, the masses will believe in clowns even if life under them is nothing but a hostile circus. This is how mediocrity comes to reign.

Supremacy virus will do anything to survive and replicate. It will mutate and migrate. Encapsulate itself in a cyst. It will burrow and go dormant. Hide deep in the folds of identity and attitude. It will flee from bone to brain and out into the ether of relationship, that bridge between souls. Can you feel this transmission? If you feel it, you can believe in it. If you believe in it, you will respect it and grant it the gravity it

13

is due. We so strongly believe in the transmission potential of the flu and its viruses, that we are threatened by someone coughing near us. We believe in it so much that we will keep our children home from school if any other child has the flu. But we do not believe in the transmission potential of supremacy virus. We will let our children play and go to school with children being raised to see our children as inferior. We will place our children in the hands of teachers and administrators who see our children as inferior. Our disbelief in supremacy's reach makes us its ally. *Believe.*

The lowest character of the least admirable of humans is an energy potential within the most admirable humans. So too is the energy potential of the most admirable person latent within the least admirable person. No people are exempt from supremacy virus, even if they have been treated as inferior for ages. We often despise this truth of intimate similarity. It rules our reality nonetheless. All living things may be infected. All may be healed.

Supremacy causes a fever so pandemic, humans experience it as natural evidence the world is well. The world is not well. Fever is the world's dire desire to heal itself. The world of living things does not want supremacy. We do. We are the infectious carrier. We uphold the lie. If nature could decide our fate, and it can, it would obliterate our caste condition, return us to dirt and prayer.

OF SLAVES AND SLAVE MASTERS

A slave makes the best slave master.
A slave master makes the best slave.

In a land of slaves and slave masters,
the spirit of both is alive in every soul.

Humans are the societal, cultural, spiritual, and ancestral children of slaves and slave masters. Acknowledging this is the first activating step in phenomenal healing. Without acknowledgment, the medicine in souls sleeps. If previous generations were citizens in a slave society, they too, in spirit, were slaves and slave masters both. One does not have to be a thing legally to have been infected by its energy spiritually. Even recent immigrants to a slavery nation, once arrived, become infected with the same illness, the same heritage. They too become slaves and slave masters. A double ailment requiring double medicine.

Slave masters have just as much healing to do as slaves. A slave master is not only the one who owns the slaves and plantation. A slave master is also the one who owns the business that benefits from slavery. The one whose children live a life that benefits from slavery. The one who will not stand up against slavery. The one who carries dehumanizing ideas of slaves. Who lives in relationship with slave masters and overseers. Who socializes with slave masters and overseers. Whose web of life is intimately intertwined with slavery. A slave master runs the schools in a slave society, teaches students the propaganda of slave society, serves lives in hospitals, shelters, and communities saturated with the values of slave society. Slave masters are anyone who contributes to the hive mind of slave society. Slave masters are everywhere.

No matter the depth of the slavery wound, its very nature is derived from the nature of the soul and its need for Love, to *be* Love. This means the slavery wound can be healed. For Love cannot be extinguished. Only suppressed for a time. That time has ended.

The greatest pain is to hate oneself. Slave masters, beneath their bravado and hostile posturing, hate themselves the most. Their soul knows its violation of the sacred law of life. It is revolted with itself, regurgitates any true inward Love.

Slaves choke for generations on seas full of hatred. But still manage to Love one another. This is Life testifying that its force is greater than hate. This is Life asserting life over what is not life. This force is in you and yours, unconditionally. For a lifetime.

The children (descendants) of slaves thrive best on daily nourishment of purposeful, focused affirmation, confirmation, celebration, and appreciation of their intrinsic beauty and worth. They need to be polished, watered, fed, and massaged, to purge the poison that comes flowing into them. And to draw into them the blessing waters that society keeps out of them. Daily, wash their spirits clean.

It is critical that slaves, to heal into freedom, continuously review their historical, humanizing, validating resume. This record includes achievements and qualifications such as: triumph, resilience, coping, dignity, resistance, risking, overcoming, enduring, creating, Loving, dreaming, flowing, growing, dying, birthing, living, giving, teaching, praying, dancing, drumming, building, helping, singing, planting, cooking, learning, longing, walking, running, shining, stunning. Slave heritage is a profound revelation of the spirit of life itself.

You cannot guilt a slave master into freeing slaves. The spirit sickness that propels a soul into mastering is immune to morality. It is a virus that cares only to perpetuate itself. It is immune to logic, guilt, compassion, shame. You waste your limited energy, focus, time, and resources trying to explain to a slave master why slavery is wrong. Your life is more effectively spent nurturing freedom in slaves, or better yet, role modeling freedom for the ones you raise.

A house slave will stand at the window in the master's home,
looking out at the field slaves toiling, and think:
Thank God I am not a slave.

Slaves become the exaggeration of all the superficial traits of their master. They call this freedom. What the master values, they value more. How the master treats people, they treat their own. If a master whips them, they whip their children. Master ways haunt the slave. The intimacy of human proximity, dependence, emotional history creates profound bonds between master and slave. They call this freedom.

Slave masters hate few things more than slaves talking about slavery. Slave masters depend on a social arrangement: slaves never talk about freedom, or about their enslavement. In return, the slave masters won't kill the slaves. At least, not so many of them.

Slave masters are the most violent of all living things. This is because they are overrun by a virus that is itself anti-life.

Only in destruction does this virus thrive. You cannot uphold an oppressive system without fostering violence in the belly of your being.

If they cannot control you, they whip you. If they cannot whip you, they chain you. If they cannot chain you, they drug you. If they cannot drug you, they imprison you. If they cannot imprison you, they kill you. If they cannot kill you, they convince you. That you are not worthy of a beautiful life.

Slave masters covet most of all the minds of the slaves. Bodies can bring value, but they wear out. Minds transmit enslavement code that can infect limitless other minds across earth and generations. Control a people's minds and you can train them to oppress themselves. They will deny themselves joy, abundance, wellness, wealth, relationship, community, creativity, bravery, peace, safety, rest, nutrition, kindness, and surely freedom. They will deny themselves their very lives.

Two slaves, starving, fought over scraps from the big house. Fought over who was on the plantation first. Fought over who had suffered more. Fought over who deserved compensation more. Fought over cultural differences and definitions. Years went by. Still fighting. In the big house, Master slept well. Because he still had slaves.

Slave masters are haunted. Malevolent spirits who seek to dominate, doom themselves to be dominated by their own existential terror. Purveyors of profound violence, they constantly fear retribution. They keep weapons close at hand. The world is a percolating violence, rendered by their ways and in their imagination. They wake in the night drenched in a cold sweat. Their nightmare is always the same: *What if people do to me and mine what we have done to them?*

To oppress a people is to be set against nature. To turn against nature is to be haunted against your own soul, which is of nature. No oppressor will ever have peace. All their apparent power is nothing. Less than an inkling of dust. Nature rules inside all of us.

Slave and slave master, oppressed and oppressor, these pairings often share an intense Love-hate, codependent relationship. They are each the most vital string holding together the life fabric that is all they have known. Such bonds can hold tight even the most toxic, destructive relations. Learn the solutions to dissolve this tragic glue.

To abuse another and be trapped in a relationship and space with them will drive you mad, turn you murderous. You are haunted by your victim who is no longer victim but testifier, truth teller, full now of intrinsic power. Every time you see them you enrage at the reminder they are. With their every glance at you, you burn at the stake of guilt and complicity. To be an oppressor is to be a tortured soul, trapped in a prison of your own making.

To live in a relationship with the one you have abused is to live in persistent guilt, shame, conflict, anger, and anxiety. This is often managed by suppressing those feelings and resenting the one you have abused, that constant reminder of your abuse. Resenting the one you have abused until all that is left in your soul is a rage fire, a desperate desire to kill and erase your constant reminder. It is hellish torture for oppressors and their favored kind to have to exist in the same society, on the same earth, as those they have oppressed. The arrangement creates in them a murderous spirit so looming they are pained to escape its shadow. No escape exists but to reckon and heal.

Slaves Love their masters with an intensity born of generational intimacy and codependence. This is not truly Love. Only obscene attachment. A bondage syndrome. But it is a force strong enough that slaves will deny their own souls for centuries. The way back to learning true Love is long. It is the only way to freedom.

Live dehumanized on a plantation or reservation long enough, and your masters and their favored kind become your North Star, your moral compass for what is okay for you to say, do, think, feel, participate in. Their approval becomes your god. Dare a new belief system. Resurrect your ancestral worship ways.

A slave family learns submissive, rationalizing ways to survive rape and abuse from slave masters and slave society. These ways are passed down generations, touching the way parents respond to the rape and abuse of themselves, and even of their own children. Recognizing how you are being violated can be a difficult ability to develop. Learning to draw boundaries around your long violated body, soul, and life can be the most challenging growth and healing of all. It is possible. Have hope. Look to the ones who have made medicine with their holy life.

An oppressed people's most prominent wound is rooted not only in the initial acts of enslavement and genocide, but also in the ongoing, generational threat to their existence. People who are not safe today struggle to heal the traumas of their yesterdays. Safe spaces are needed in this Love work you do.

For oppressors, their most severe wound is born of a collective experience with being part of a social cultural body engaged in dehumanizing others who are in fact human. It is reasonable to say that the most traumatized and tortured humans of all are the offspring generations of oppressors. Charged with preserving their family and cultural legacy of supremacy and all its entitlements and privileges so woven into their identity. They are contorted by the burden and conflict in their soul. They dare not peer honestly into what they are upholding. Yet their being is dying to be a human being.

The idea of benefitting others does not appeal to a soul infected with and overrun by slavery virus. Masters care only for their own benefit, and for that of those with whom they identify. Slaves, in a panic of despair, only care for their benefit, and that of those they believe can benefit them. Find other motives besides charity to persuade souls toward freedom.

Slave masters are strange farmers. They farm suffered silence, obedience, fear, collusion, conformity. This is all they care to bring to the market. They are not organic farmers. They will use poison to kill anything that threatens their crop.

Many slaves detest the idea of freedom. They have been conditioned for generations. The scent of fear lives in their bones. Don't wait on slaves to free you. You must do the work of freeing yourself.

Freedom requires a way of life that allows you to be centered, still inside, balanced, and secure. Slave masters seed calculated chaos and instability. They know this will unleash fear. After a dose of fear, most slaves want to run back into their chains. Prepare an oasis inside your soul and in your life. Center yourself there.

If you stop the master from whipping you, the master feels persecuted. If you stop laboring for the master, the master feels oppressed. If you reclaim your original names for people and places from the master's colonizing renaming, the master feels vandalized. If you return the master's land to the people the master stole it from, the master feels terrorized. If you return the master's wealth, resources, and freedoms to those whose labor generated it, the master feels violated. If you and your people choose freedom, the master feels enslaved. Do not put the master's feelings and reactions at the center of your revolution. The master's moral compass was broken from the very beginning.

Slave masters do everything they care to with the bodies, minds, hearts, labor, and creative life of slaves, except examine the horror of enslaving them. Denial is their way of life. Truth burns their eyes.

Do not ask. Do not wait. Do not explain.
Choose. Choose freedom.

You cannot reason with a slave master. If you wait for the slave master to set free the slaves you will wait forever. If you find a thousand brilliant ways to ask for freedom, your request will never be granted. If you explain your freedom rights with genius clarity, your explanation will be wasted in the wind. Your energy is better spent breaking free. And working with others to generate collective freedom conditions.

It deeply grieves a slave to offend the master. A slave will destroy other slaves before disappointing the master. Oppression lives most of all not between master and slave, but between slave and slave. Generational oppression is raised through intimate relations.

Slave language is self-defeating, self-incarcerating, fear-drenched, and yet hope remains within it. Like panning for gold in a stream, you can filter hope gold from slave language if you take great care to examine it in natural lighting. You can extract the original beauty.

Slave master language is self-rationalizing, self-justifying, soaked in defensive fear, as though the slave master is under unjust assault from every direction. Siphon this language through its root language of terrified suffering. See what meaning emerges from the wailing.

Being a slave master or slave is a choice. No matter the degree of infection. The soul is more powerful than this virus can ever be. It will triumph when and where it is called to prevail.

One day a family of slaves was granted a chance to express their grievances to the slave master and his wife. As the slaves spoke, at times fearfully and timidly, sometimes with ancestral strength, the slave master grew defensive. His wife started crying. The meeting ended abruptly. The next day, the slave master said to the slave family, *I thought we were all getting along so well before. Look at all we have done for you. Last night my wife and I were feeling guilty about what you told us. My wife was upset. It's not fair that you should cause us guilt and distress. Try to focus on the positive in life and don't be a disruption. We're all one family here. We don't see differences. This is a peaceful plantation. If you hate it, maybe you should go back to where you came from.* After the master left the slave quarters, the slave family felt badly about the guilt and distress they had caused the master and his wife. They couldn't go back to where they came from. They knew Master depended too much on their free labor and wouldn't let them leave. Also because they had no way back, no longer knew where they were stolen from, and this was the only land and life they had known. They just wanted freedom in *this* land. They never brought up their grievances again. They were sleepless for many nights after that, feeling guilty for having upset Master and his wife. During those same nights, Master and his wife slept peacefully. For they still had slaves.

OPPRESSION WAYS

First the world oppresses us.
Then we oppress our own soul.
Then we oppress the world.

Your oppressors do not want you to believe oppression exists. This is your oppressors' greatest power against you: the idea that the conditions of your life and those you Love are a matter of fact, just in their nature, and of your destiny. Your oppressors are full-time slaves. Slaves to a need to convince you your life is as it is supposed to be and you can do nothing about it. Your oppressors think about this night and day, without pause, for your oppressors sense that the moment this effort is paused, truth will seep into your life and you will begin to believe your oppression is real. Your oppressors are terrified of this. They need you to believe in the lies, myths, fables, fantasies they pass from generation to generation of their own children, and yours.

Do not spend your precious energy, gifts, time, and focus trying to convince your oppressors that your oppression is real. You can present all the data you want. They will never see your cause as valid. They know you are oppressed. They just don't want you and yours to know you are oppressed or to respond to your oppression with a certainty of its injustice. As long as they keep you in doubt, they keep you in chains, and benefit from your indentured, incarcerated labor.

If you ask your oppressors for freedom, they will say you already have it. They will shame you for asking. They will call you disruptive, angry, a negative influence on the agreed-to social peace. They will ask you to slow down. *Speed up.* Not into an anxious, rushed speed. Into a purposeful, steady, *nowness.* Move, Revolutionary. Move.

Beware those who lie perpetually and rant of the truth being a lie. They are the drum major for supremacy and oppression. They are the bugle boy sent out to rally a lost cause and bully the slaves back into their shackles. They bang a drum that has no soul.

Call someone a degrading word long enough and if they aren't being nurtured with truth, they will become that word. They will use it on themselves, yet still consider themselves liberated, enlightened, conscious, awakened. Even as their generations suckle the teat of degradation, living lives satisfying the fantasy of their oppressor.

You will know oppressors and deniers by the profound constipation of their soul. Tense, tight faces and bodies. Grimacing on occasions of joy and celebration. Often unable to sing or dance or find rhythm with the natural world they have vacated for their supremacy throne.

The endpoint of materialism and individualism is resource exhaustion and social collapse. Conditions ripe for the resurgence of supremacy, dehumanization, and oppression. A callous circle. As an oppressor, you deplete souls, so they are tempted to deplete the world. Deplete the world, so souls are tempted to deplete themselves of soul and sacredness. *Everyone for themselves.* This is a theme pleasing to the ears of oppression.

People raised in supremacy are consumed with believing they are good people, that the society rendered in their image is supreme. They have a need to call their society *Number One, the best in the world, advanced,* and *First World.* A river of insecurity flows beneath this need. An insecurity that comes from existing in and upholding an unnatural and artificial order that favors and entitles them.

Oppressors are trapped in an obsession: to render themselves invisible in the public eye as the cause of oppression. They succeed by having society never identify the culprit. We call people oppressed, marginalized, underserved, dehumanized, impoverished. But we never say by whom. Oppressed by whom? Marginalized by whom? Underserved by whom? Dehumanized by whom? Oppressors succeed in convincing themselves they are good, righteous, superior people. They succeed by creating cultural blindness to their existence and their destructive pathology. To overcome this collective blindness, drag the sickness out into the light. Name it over and again. Identify its instances. Point out its workings. Trace its history in bold ink. Teach the children how people arrive into their collective condition. Reveal the caste system. Explain the origins of the social order. This is how you destroy that order.

Oppressors will project onto oppressed people all of their own foul traits. This is how they protect their identity and justify their oppressive ways. If they are lazy in exploiting your labor, they will call you lazy. If they live on oppression entitlements, they will say your people are always seeking handouts, undeserved benefits. If they are violent toward your people, they will say your people are naturally violent. If they are uncivilized toward you, they will call you uncivilized. If they are savage toward you, they will call you savages. If they are unclean, unintelligent, unqualified for their social station, they will cast you as all these things. They will build these ideas about your people into a fortress lasting generations. They will exist in this fortress and it will defend them from the truth. It will hold their supremacy lie in place, a rancid caulking resistant to the rains of shame and guilt. In fact, any shame and guilt they begin to feel only hardens the caulking, fortifying their long, ultimately doomed season of manufactured supremacy.

It is malevolent, strategic hypocrisy when societies built on the death of freedom celebrate freedom, call themselves lands of freedom, fill their propaganda with freedom words. See this hypocrisy. It holds your freedom.

Accelerated pace of life is an oppression tool. To move toward freedom, slow your pace. Rejoin all the sacredness found at your center: Love. Spirit. Soul. Ancestors. Intuition. Discernment. Seeing. Hearing. Feeling. Healing. Growing. Purpose. Passion. Creativity. Inspiration. Humility. Grace. Patience. Hope. Openness. Renewal.

Their entire lives, oppressors will live, work, socialize, worship with their kind, then claim to be blind to the distinctions of those who are not their kind. *I don't see differences.* This is their tired, dishonest mantra. In this way they erase you and avoid reckoning with the virus in them. Such will be their pained discomfort with your existence and presence that they will shoot at you a thousand arrows of aggression in your daily encounters. They will claim to be your friend even as they assault and erode your humanness.

They will say that by speaking of freedom you disturb the peace. But they disturbed the peace when they came for your lands, your bodies, your labor, your language and worship and ceremonies, your children and dreams, your ancestors and memories. They continue disturbing the peace, for they cannot stop taking. So, please, speak of freedom. Disturb every fraudulent peace.

They will project onto you every character flaw they can grasp to justify their belief in your inferiority. They will have a dire need to be at the center of the circle. Any circle. They will experience loss of entitlement as a grave unfairness, an injustice needing a raging response. They will weaponize their anger and tears against any attempt to discuss or address the conditions that keep them in a place of superiority, power, and control. Their emotional offense will be as a pot lid keeping the simmering discontent of the oppressed from boiling over into revolt.

Many peoples have been divided and picked off on the road to liberation. This is how hyenas hunt. Study their tactics. Become geniuses at staying closely woven. You cannot afford to leak water on your way across the desert. And if you cannot achieve or maintain solidarity, at least do not devour one another. Eat other things.

The surest way to identify your oppressor is to call out your oppression. Uninfected souls will want you to be free and will appreciate or at least respect your grievance. Your oppressors will resent you for saying you are oppressed.

They know they are the source. Sickness doesn't like being called sick.

If they resent you thriving soulfully, what are they?
Identify their species.

Avoid debating those who prefer to keep your people down. You lose so much finite energy, time, and focus this way. Stay in your freedom garden, turning ground, planting seeds, watering precious souls.

Freedom is not a thing you ask for from your oppressor. It is something you grow and harvest in your own soul. Oppressors and their favored kind have less than no authority in certifying that an unfavored people are free. Only those people can say whether they are free. The measurement happens in the soul.

Submission is an objective of oppression. Your oppressor trains you to fear what happens if you don't submit. To fear this more than you fear the cost you pay for submitting. You learn to think it natural to submit even your body, hair, and language for inspection by your master. Submissive as ever, you submit your thoughts and feelings for approval. Your life becomes an endless application for acceptance. Not into Love. Into deathly bondage.

Fear. Guilt. Shame. Amnesia. Silence. Your need to please. All of these are weapons your oppressors uses against you and your people to keep you down. They use medicine, research, resources, technology, media, law, miseducation, manipulated history, sacred scripts, everything against you. All while exclaiming it is for you. These are their instruments of control. To weaken, discourage, confuse, and divide you. Care enough to remember, recreate, and hold sovereign your own ways.

Oppressors see themselves as generous, benevolent, and compassionate for *allowing* unfavored people into their superior spaces and stolen wealth. This creates in oppressors a resentment that unfavored people have been given so much and yet still complain, still will not do for themselves. This narrative is the bedtime story oppressors read their children, raising them to be oppressors.

Slave masters Love to sit on the big house porch, sipping drinks, watching the slaves labor themselves to death in the heat, and call the slaves *good for nothing* and *lazy*. Irony and hypocrisy are common minerals in the soil and soul of oppressive society.

Whatever *favors* oppressors dole out to unfavored people become code language for unjust benefits, while masking the truly unjust benefits upon which oppressors build their supremacy life. What oppressors call unfavored people is a sheer reflection of qualities within oppressors themselves. *Lazy, hysterical, hypersexual, dirty, unintelligent, primitive...* Even as oppressors cast these stones, the same stones accumulated most often in the character of those who oppress.

Your people are hardworking, so they call you lazy. Brilliant so they call you unintelligent. Speak in your ancestral language structure, so they call you inarticulate. Are affectionate with each other and kind to strangers, so they call you violent. Passionate, so they call you angry. Close with nature, so they call you savage. Advanced with your ancestral knowing, so they call you primitive. All that you are, they will call you the opposite, poisoning the whole world and ongoing generations with lies about you. They are a house of horrors filled with mirrors that lie. If you live in their world, you pass through their soul and its tortured imagination of themselves and you.

Do not wait on your oppressor to stop oppressing you.
They don't want enlightenment.
They want you oppressed.

They will pressure you to wait for your freedom. Don't wait. You will be waiting for eternity. They will say it is too soon. Soon it will be too late. They will say change takes time. Your people have been dying forever. Forever is time enough. They will ask you not to shut them out from your revolution. Their denial and avoidance is the door that shuts them out. Persist with your revolution. They will want you to make your revolution more comfortable for them. Their comfort has enslaved your kind all along. Revolution is truth. Truth is not polite. It is necessary. Comfort has nothing to do with it.

They will say you threaten their way of life. But their way of life is death. You cannot oppress life and reap life. Your revolution threatens their way of death. Remember this. *Remember who you are.* Remember Spirit that fills you with life. Remember your ancestors. Remember what you are here for. To live. Not to approximate living. Not to prepare to live. Not to hope to live or dream of living. You are here to live. Which is to be free. Spend as much time as possible around free living things. Let their ways influence you.

If they pressure you to proclaim you are free, your people are free, your society is free, this is oppression. Through their systemic, collective pressure, they disprove their own point.

31

Being expected to serve as the great illuminator, explainer, validator, or healer of your own oppressor is itself a sign of a slave-slave master relational habit. Do not dance for your terrorizer. Don't do that jig.

They will slander your character, relations, methods, motives, even your dreams. Do not become consumed by their arrows, for those arrows will be unceasing. Let Spirit direct your revolution. If you fall into a reactive existence, your oppressors will take command of your revolution, take it to deep water, and drown it.

They will begin killing you. Murder is the true heart of an oppressor. When they begin killing you, go out to the living world and testify. Send out your record through the animals, plants, children, and healers and creators. Let them know why the killing happened. What your response will be. Your response will be revolution.

Extreme individualism is an instrument of oppression. It creates existential anxiety, fear, insecurity, greed, and the lust for false power and false control. Supremacy and inferiority crave the climate conditions that cause people to believe they exist separate from the world, separate from any duty to living things. When you lose hold of the rope of collective relationship, you experience a sensation of falling, plummeting to your death. Supremacy wants you to lose the rope. Hold on. Hold your people in your heart and way of life.

Many of your oppressors do not realize they are your oppressors. They may look like you. Or they may be offspring or descendants of earlier oppressors, raised to believe this way of being is natural and just. They may be unware of the virus breeding in them, and the harm it is doing in the world. These unaware oppressors may be the most dangerous of all, for they are liable to take violent offense to the suggestion that they are an oppressor, that they are anything other than a good person. Be willing to burst their goodness bubble. It is not just a bubble. It is a sanctuary for oppressors.

When a parent confronts the truth of a child's unwellness and harmfulness, and does not enable those things, we say that is a parent who Loves the child. When a person confronts a society's unwellness and harmfulness, and does not enable those things, oppressors do not say that is a person who Loves the country. They say that is a person who hates the country. This is how supremacy protects its illegitimate place and system. By invalidating and recasting the revolutionary as an enemy of the people. Do not fall for this old manipulation. Do not fall. Rise.

When a scientist discovers or develops an insight or technique useful to medical wellbeing, that person is hailed and celebrated for bringing about revolutionary change. When oppressed people strive for systemic change that would begin to alleviate the social ills of their people, they too are labeled and treated as terrorists by the true terrorists who trade in oppression. Revolutionaries are ghosts who haunt mainstream minds and the status quo those minds support.

Many people boast of being patriots even as they reek of hate and disdain for the oppressed of the country they claim to Love. You cannot hate part of the land and rightfully claim to Love the land. You cannot despise and resent some of the people and brag of being a patriot. A patriot is a Lover and defender of the entire land, the entire people, the whole fruit of the freedom tree. A true patriot will deny the government if the government acts against any of the people, for a patriot is of the people. Not some of the people. Not people similar to the patriot. All the people. A patriot swallows the bitter and the sweet. Defends the principle of collective good. Is loyal not to a political position or group but to the positionless aura of Love. A patriot disappoints fanatics. Is unsatisfying to partisans. Lives as an enigma to popular trends. People cannot trust a patriot to be on their side, for a patriot is sideless. But when those people drop their siding and move naked into the honoring of souls, they may trust a patriot above all else. For a patriot is given to freedom's unconditional cause.

They will tell you, *Don't talk about it. You will only cause division.* But all healing requires attention. We must raise our children to talk about it. To examine it and speak of what is found. No sickness wants to confront itself. Healing by nature Loves the mirror of truth.

When your kind begins to rise into freedom, your oppressors will begin to experience a profound grief. An immense sense of loss. They will mourn for the days when they didn't have to see your kind in their exclusive spaces. Didn't have to consider your kind, hear your voices, include your perspective. When they could treat your kind however they wished, could exploit, abuse, kill, and erase your kind without any consequence or sanction. They miss those *greater glory days*. They grieve the loss of unjust power and control, the days when their lie and life of supremacy went unchallenged. For those who want to see their favored kind become more human, they must treat their favored kind's grief as a real suffering. For you who want freedom for your kind, treat your oppressors' grief as a real suffering. If not, your revolution will underestimate the energy you are up against. Their mourning will eclipse your freedom morning. Stay in your sun.

SOUL OF A REVOLUTIONARY

If your soul is on fire to serve in a way that scares you to death. And you don't feel worthy, ready, able. And the burning will not leave you alone. Congratulations. You have your calling. Bless you. Your life is not for you. It is for the world. This is an ancestral arrangement. You've already been promised as an offering. If you can follow your heart and spirit, even through fear, not only can you fulfill your own soul and harvest a profound peace, you can also be medicine for all living things. All your relations.

What did I come here for?
Answer this every day of your life.

Why am I here? This is a question that can bring you to life. When you feel you are dying of mundane, surrendered malaise. Dying of fear and confusion. Dying from constant fleeing. Ask yourself, *Why am I here?* Ask it from your chest and gut. Answer with whatever courage you can muster. The answer can light your weakened embers. May even cause a bonfire in time.

to feel it all

When your reasons for speaking and living in truth overcome your reasons for staying silent, you become a revolutionary. Each day, parts of you die for many causes. Of the dyings you choose, ensure you die for beautiful things. If you want freedom, you will have to die endlessly. And you will have to be born endlessly. This is a matter of losing your attachment chains. You are birthing a new world. Birth labor is painful. Find reason, will, and courage to push this new world out through you.

A revolution is first an *in-rising* before it is an uprising. The soul within must reject its imposed and accepted oppressive reality. Then it must rise within, forcing a person into outward cause and action. Soul rebellion precedes social rebellion. Which is why the first and last revolution work occurs in the soul.

The most effective revolutionaries first wage revolution in their own souls. They come alive encountering their intangible persona, cry joy at the opportunity to purge their inner sediment. They realize to live lukewarm is not living. A certain heat is required for waking into illumination's dream. Freedom is a fire burning deep in your soul. It does not spend its time with mediocrity. The soul of your soul wants freedom. Above all, want your own soul. That way, you can never be denied.

People believe they need a leader. They need permission. Help them wake the permission that is their soul. They will lead themselves.

Your revolution grows first and most vitally in the people, the pueblo, not in iconic leadership. Without common devotion, soul work, and action, rarified personas have no soil for their particular seed. The people are the heart and spirit of revolution. They are the carriers, the oxygen to keep alive the flame. They need ceaseless nurturing for such arduous weather. Soul food in every form.

Moments may come when you feel like a fraud in your revolution. People will savor the chance to reveal you as a fraud. If you stay a spout of your divine source, you cannot be fraudulent. You will be imperfect. This does not disqualify your revolution or you as revolutionary. Be a fountain of

Love. This will be your excellence. Which is sufficient for what freedom asks.

At times a revolution is a white water river, rampant with churning social attention, conformity pressures, and human dramas. At such times, it can be difficult to see clearly, feel clearly, think clearly. It can be hard to stay in spirit discernment. Other times, a revolution is a slow, underground seeping, with little visible evidence of progress or notable rewards. Here is when doubt can sprout and spread like hillside weeds. Silence is a virtue and gift in revolution. An oasis for retreat. Even in the stretches of river rapids, give yourself to silence. It will answer questions and solve impossible crises. Silence will give you peace and the power of seeing. It will show you the way.

Maybe you feel comfortable in your life, and the last thing you want is to be a revolutionary. Maybe that feels like too much work, too many risks, too many sacrifices and dangers. But if you are burning inside for freedom, you may have no choice. For if you are called and do not answer, surely you will suffer a terrible emptiness. An unfulfillment that haunts your lifetime.

The question is not: *Am I ready for revolution?* The question is: *Am I ready for what life will be without revolution?* People do not revolt for amusement. They are left no choice. Revolutionaries despise the reality that forces them into revolution. They would rather an easier life.

It is unbearable to live as prey inside an entire people's psychosis for generations, centuries. Unbearable. Still, you bear it. But it costs you. Who, treated as a monster for generations, manages not to become a monster? Only those who confront the monster. And who confront the monstering in themselves.

Do not expect to join your kind in the Promised Land. Not in your living body form. To expect this is to bind the revolution to your selfhood. Selfhood is a killer of revolutions. Think and sow and sorrow in a vision of generations. See the glory of your people as an eternal river. Hold this sacred dream. Drink from it daily. Your people don't need heroes in bodies walking them to freedom. They need spirit in all things, transforming them there.

Keep your revolution work and identity spread out in ownership among the people, not concentrated in and associated with select personas. When your revolution is concentrated, it is easier to suppress. You just remove or defame the icons. When the masses own their revolution, they are millions of fires burning for new life. It is not so easy to put all these fires out. Spread your fire. Make your revolution about you, and you lose it. Make it about all living things, and it erupts into purposeful glory. Make your revolution a passion garden. Invite everyone to get down and dirty.

A revolution has moods. Freedom doesn't always want the same food. Pay attention to the moment. Burn all your scripts and bear witness. Follow the collective spirit. No need to predetermine every step. Sometimes change enjoys and flourishes with a freestyle music.

Possessiveness will flare up within your revolution. Separation and antagonism. Selfish ideas will emerge, whispering that subgroups and spaces need not touch or matter to one another. These ideas are untrue and destructive. Oppression virus has no boundary. It is a powerful transient that cannot be contained. Only Spirit can annihilate the self into *Allness*. Only *Allness* douses the fire of possessive pride. Keep your revolution saturated in sacred spirit that bows to the inseparable web of life.

People will judge, convict, condemn, and crucify you. Sometimes especially those closest to you. They are projecting their inner nightmare on to your sweet soul dream. People can only imagine you. Leave them to their dream. Love regardless. Be Love. Only you can truly know you. Live inside that miracle. Be what you came here to be. All living things are counting on you to be you. This is how we keep harmony and light in the world. By being true. Regardless. Bless you. And all your relations. All things are your relations.

They will try to bleach your essence from your soul.
They will try to bleach your name,
your tongue, your truth, your culture.
Stay all your wondrous colors. Paint this world in you.

Your journey is not to become like everyone else. No one is like everyone else. Your journey is to live completely exposed to life and still retain the qualities of your personal phenomenon. You aren't here to satisfy. You are here to add a particular seasoning to our collective stew. You marinated in the moments and marrow of your ancestors. You were ready at your first spark. When doubt and fear rise up in you, see them, greet them, invite them on their way. This is not when you turn and run. This is when you root and romance the soul of your soul. In your deepest dreams wakes a whisper: *I want to be myself*. Bring this whisper into your conscious life. Sing it as a song. Dance your wildest euphoria. If you can learn who you are and celebrate it with the passion of birth, you will be free. And everything you set your eyes upon will blush afire with your soulful artistry.

They will say you are divisive for speaking against oppression and injustice. Oppression and injustice are divisive. They stay alive by silencing you. Don't worry about unity. Worry about truth. Empowerment. Healing. Freedom doesn't care who disagrees with it.

You may say it is too much trouble for you to place yourself in freedom's fire, to stand in this work. But have you measured the toll on you, living a daily life targeted by hostility, aggression, violence, lack of safety and affection? These energies come from your oppressors' eyes and attitudes as much as their words and actions. You are a sacred moon deeply marked, scarred, and eroded by this constant rain of terror and malice. Have you come to accept this exhausting existence as normal life? Then they own you. You have embraced genocide of your kind as an inevitable aspect of the climate. Measured against this assault, is freedom's fire truly too much trouble?

They will attack your memory ceaselessly. They will pit you against your recollection of your own history, your accounting of your own experience. They will come for your story, history, faith, language, children, leaders, followers. They will come for everyone. Inside their wrath, you will only be acceptable to them in docility, silence, and self-blame for your own suffering. Even in the heat of daytime, slave quarters are cold with the chill of internalized shame.

The climate change that will preserve earth and nature is the climate change inside human souls. Your work is soul work. Soul work prepares the mind to be fertile for freedom ideas and fallow for oppression ideas. Effective revolutionaries take on qualities of the soul. They are the image of that essence in which they spend their time and lives.

You know those people who are excited at the beginning of a project, when ideas are grand and hope is high. Soon, their enthusiasm wanes, their contributions lessen. Then they don't show up at all. Freedom is such a project. Many souls will fall away over the course of your revolution. They are excited by immediate, easy shows of rebellion, but falter at the thought of a long journey of sacrifice and labor. Let such souls come and go in this work. They have their particular value. All spices season a stew. Nurture closely those who endure the way. In their endurance is the answer to why freedom matters. Living things will live underground for decades for the chance to fulfill their calling in the light of sun.

Praise can lift you. It can also bloat your idea of you and set you adrift from your revolution. When you find yourself drifting, follow your people's pain back home. To lead a revolution, die each day into humility and grace. To follow revolutionary leadership, die each day into your own revolutionary power. Burn away your identity as helpless and unworthy. Daily ceremonies and true relations can help.

If you are a revolutionary, a fire has been burning in you all your life. Feed it. Feed it not the detritus of common corrupted life. Feed it the precious elements forever flowing through the luminous dimension within common life. Feed it whatever beauty nourished your ancestors. Arrive to that harvest by turning your Love inward. Let it serrate your spirit and reach the yolk that is your soul. Your soul carries all the beauty of all times and before time. Your soul is your genealogical library and library access card, all at once.

Some can't help going first into the fire. These are revolutionaries. Others are more than willing to follow. They drink the sacred water revolutionaries leave in their wake, then become something of that essence. Some of them even become great revolutionaries. They bloom late. And some wait until no other choice exists before plunging. Even as they join, they are terrorized, paralyzed, panicked. But they jump. Do not keep a list on the order of arrival to your revolution. This order can be deceiving. Keep tuned to who is in the fire. All souls can be kindling for freedom.

In one way, few souls are revolutionaries, caught up in a current of resistance and triumph stronger than the current of fear. In another way, every soul is a revolutionary. To live, to remain alive, is to revolt against dying and death. This instinct, this impulse can be buried by the mixture of fear and social conditioning. Collective human life, when not rooted in soulfulness, can be an atmosphere that kills the revolutionary spirit, and kills revolutionaries. The labor and life you seek is a soulful one.

As you lead revolt, they come for you, to splice you from your people. And from yourself. If their voice or nature becomes your god, you have lost your god and your revolution. When they come for you, and they will, do not close. Open. Open like the sky. Open, in Love, to your people, ancestors, and Great Spirit. Open to the pain inside the rage with which they come for you. Open to the generational destiny of supremacy and oppression now surging against you, a tide of karma and conclusion. *Open.*

If you stand, speak, act for freedom, they will come for you.
Who? They who are terrified of freedom.

First they will ignore you. Then they will laugh at you. Then they will curse and scold you. They will create slanderous stories about you, bullying others to shun you. They will come for those closest to you, pushing them to betray you. Finally, they will light their torches, look at each other for approval, and come for you. In seeking to devour the light you offer, they will devour the last flickering of light in themselves. They believe that by removing you, they remove their greatest threat. Instead, in removing you, they liberate your message into the ether, and unleash their greatest threat, which is the poisoning in their soul. As they destroy what they fear, they metastasize the cancer in their bones that was waiting only for a final act of aggression to break free and saturate their blood and being. They kill themselves.

Some revolutionaries choose not to stay on the plantation to try to change it. They lead their kindred ones off the plantation, to choose new land. Other revolutionaries stay on the plantation and work to heal the land, water, air, spirit, and souls. Both kinds of freedom workers are vital to a revolution. The revolutions that become legendary in human memory reach everywhere, touch everything.

As your radiance grows, more souls will be drawn to you. You are not here to feed their hunger. You are here to feed your light. Subtle difference on the sacred path. Stay free. Don't become a fatal offering for someone's ravenous, misled appetite. You are not obligated. They can truly feed themselves. You must feed your light. So it may remain candling in the world. The right ones will cherish, honor, and be nourished by your light without devouring you.

Avoid the seductive idea of being royalty. What is the sacred value of placing yourself higher than others? What does your soul gain from having people bow and kneel to you, kiss your feet and worship your robes? You do not have to be a queen or king, princess or prince ruling the world. Be a humble peasant and rule over peace in your soul. What tragedy for you to seek to rise up out of slavery by crowning yourself a master over other slaves. It is not necessary to carry royal titles to live and shine in a regal way. If you have royal aspirations, you drank them from the cup your oppressor poured. Now your bones believe royalty is some

43

peak achievement, some divine quality. You can feel better about yourself without calling yourself supreme. You can heal your sense of inferiority and powerlessness without sitting on thrones and demeaning those without a throne. Crowns and thrones are symbols that say, *You are less than me.* Destroy those fraudulent symbols of insecurity. The greatest living things live nakedly. No need to look for people to bow to your brilliance. Open your heart to the miracle of humility. Let your brilliance take its own bows. In the end, royalty will not make your soul shine or your life complete. Find your path by staying close to earth. Let the ground of communion dose you with the specialness you seek.

People create idols in their revolutions. Work earnestly to kill the weeds of idolization before they mature. Otherwise, your people will eventually kill their idols. If you are one of those idols, your people's pain will turn on you like a wildfire. You will be their outlet for destruction when they cannot destroy their enslaver or the pain of their enslavement. Heroes are illusionary personas not even the hero can live up to. If your revolution lives in heroes, it will die with the fall of those heroes. Keep your revolution with the people. Even if they don't feel worthy. Don't let their inner disbelief decide the revolution. Stay in the soil where things bow down each day.

Dear Soul, do not let anyone idolize you.
After the compliment comes the crucifixion.

As soon as you become an idol to someone, you are no longer a person to them. No longer allowed to change, grow, fail, misstep, feel, be hurt, grow tired, have needs, be fed and nurtured. Now you are an inert object to be used by the needful diversion, escapism, and vicarious imagining of the idolizer. You are held higher than is possible to exist, flattened out of your multidimensional nature into a one-dimensional idea. A caricature. Expectations are built around you into a prison that keeps you inside ideals and fantasies. Praise is fickle. Don't sell your soul for that easy trinket. People will, with the same passion, praise you and then raze you, tear you down in a demolition of resentment and disappointment. Don't get intoxicated on the heights of praise. You will be in no condition to endure the scorn to follow. Many souls drive drunk on praise only to fall asleep at the humbling wheel of reality. Stay human. Compliments that feel like a person is separating and elevating you from them are precursors to the violence many do to foreign things. Allowing people to put you on a pedestal is as self-harming as allowing them to abuse you. Stay on the ground in the rich soil of your imperfection. Touch and taste your wild roots and remain forested in Grace. May all your relationships be filled with mutual honor. May you stay free in the way you see yourself. Free in the way you exist with others. Free in the way you uniquely roam this sufficient earth.

You will gain disciples even if you do not wish for them. Stay in your spirit as you reflect on your relationship with them. They will be drawn to you each for their own reasons. Some are cold and dim in the soul and want your heat and light. Some want the attention others fix on you. Some want to be close, to feed and protect you. Others want to be close, to betray you. So they can say they know your true nature and secrets. So they can end your revolution. Some will see you as teacher. Resist being their guru. Encourage them to guru themselves. Some will want to teach you. Search your soul for how you can be their student. Some want you in their gossip, or gossiping with them. Some are curious about your apparent singularity, about why you won't conform. All your disciples bring their own lives and wounds and hopes with them. They bring all their people and generations. Take this lightly, and you harm the revolution. Take it sacredly, and among these souls will be ones who carry forward the revolution fire.

A strong wind sweeps you up into the sky of social applause. But the ground below is where you were made fruitful. Down in the soil of humility where the healing roots and herbs grow. This is a story about staying close to what strengthens you. Freedom's sky is not above you. It is in you. A rich bed for what you need. Do not grow inebriated on praise or dissuaded by hostility. Revolutions breathe well in the air of sobriety, humility, and abundant hopefulness.

You are a painter. In your lifetime, your paintings are regarded as a common thing. Some people resent your work. Some see its beauty and secrets. After your lifetime, the value of your work comes to light in certain circles, grows more understood. Maybe it is celebrated. Its secrets spill out for the eyes made to recognize them. Which is enough. This is how it is with your freedom work. It is not for you. It is not for your time. It is a painting whose gift is deciphered by the eyes of the ages.

If you cannot hear the drum of justice beating in your weary spirit, it is not because the drum is not there or is not sounding. Your drum-deafness is a condition of your soul, not of the drum. This is a hopeful truth. When we speak of justice here, we mean not retribution, compensation, or comeuppance. We mean the fulfillment of the course of natural life. We mean freedom.

Don't be afraid to do it your way.

For every area of your life, fulfillment, peace, and joy are waiting for you on the other side of doing it your way. Fear of doing it your own way is one of the most crippling impediments to a beautiful life. Conformity pressure is a bully. A potent seed for oppression. A gravitational force that holds you close to mediocrity and dissatisfaction. When you avoid doing it your way, you deny the world what you came here for. You aren't here to conform. You are here to enlighten the norm. You are literally a born revolutionary. Touch your conformity roots daily. You will see they are inherited. Not native to you. Your ancestors prayed a child would come who at last broke the chains of their bondage. *You are that one.* Touch your conformity roots. Lift them from your soul. Let them go. You, and your life, and your sacred offering are so much more beautiful when you do it your way.

Stay whole.
That's your revolution.

Who you are. You don't have to defend it. Or explain it. You just have to set it free. That's your journey. In the end, you will not count the souls who understood you. You will ponder the soulfulness with which you lived your life. You will want to feel you tasted often your own wilderness. And it was divine.

NATURE OF FREEDOM

A naked, diaphanous figure is dancing everywhere you look. You can barely bare its beauty, a radiance so impossible that tears spring from your soul spring when you glance at its aura. You fall so in Love you spend your whole life trying to possess this miracle. This nascent light in every corner. You adhere to all the rules passed down to you. You follow all the approved paths, even when it breaks your heart. You achieve all the expected achievements. You acquire all the titles, relationships, and status. Yet the divine candlelight keeps taunting you, dancing closer, then further away. You feel its warmth against your pleading skin, but it draws back and leaves you cold. You spend your life pleasing what humans want from you, losing touch with true pleasure assigned to you by Glory. You become a searcher, a wanderer, a traveling ache. You renounce pleasure and romance, start digging in the hard desert earth for the nakedness of your obsession. Years go by. Decades. You feel you have been cheated. You rebel against all rules. You rebel against your soul. Your gamble is that if you perform anarchy against life, you will finally possess this effervescent creature for yourself. Nothing works. The dancing ecstasy comes into you and out of you in flashes of euphoria and torture. At last, one day, when your yearning has grown exhausted, you collapse into a kind of surrender. You fall into the boiling vat of your own soul water, which has been within you all along. The *you* of you gets cooked. Old bindings come undone. You are rearranged into particles of light. Your seven senses die into a new sense that makes no sense. You are born into the same body, the same world, but everything now is breeze and movement. The dancing form you always sought is nowhere to be found. But you are dancing. You no longer care about the music or the beat. Your dance is bliss without boundary. Pains come and go. You stay dancing. Your ideas die as soon as they form in you. Great Sky above calls you *Friend* and joins you dancing. This, dear soul, is freedom.

Study the soul and psychology of freedom. It will serve you well. Oppression is not magic. It is not unpredictable or unexplainable. When you know the nature of human beings, and understand the human condition, it dawns on you that oppression is the most unoriginal, uninspired of things. Freedom is not a favor granted or received. It is the persona of life. Seek to be *alive* while you are alive.

Freedom has a fragrance. Those who have known freedom recognize its fragrance on living things. If you are lost from freedom, go to something that is free and learn the scent of its wildness. See how it smells on your skin. Freedom smells differently on each soul. Your musk is always enhanced by freedom cologne. Exude it and you attract life to you.

A mystic kind of sugar sweetens freedom tea.

Water will show you what freedom is. Try to destroy it and it changes form but retains its essence. Swallow it and you become it. Bottle it and it maintains its grace. Pollute it and it remains open to being cleansed. Feed it to living things and they grow more alive. Your soul too can be water for the world.

Many people say, *As soon as I have freedom in the world, then I can be free in my soul.* Freedom does not work this way. Without freedom in your soul you cannot have freedom in the world. Give a soulfully homeless person a house and they are still homeless inside. Only when a soul becomes *homeful* can that person end their physical homelessness. Only when you liberate your soul can you become free out among souls. If strife is a cage, breath is the door. Freedom is you breathing beautifully. When you learn to turn your pain into power, your power into peace, now you are free.

Sovereignty is not only a quality of self-determination. A people, together, must also determine to be sovereign. Social agreements are renewed and rewritten every day. A purposeful revolution petitions souls to ask within the sacred circle, *What do we agree to today?*

You know wind by what it moves.
You know freedom by the way it moves your soul.

If you watch a leaf on water closely, you see their two natures figuring out how to be with each other. This is freedom.

Freedom is not a secret. Freedom is everywhere. *We* are the secret. All other living things talk among themselves about us, asking, *How is it that with all their blessings, still they are not free?* Fear is the seed. Supremacy and inferiority are the roots. Oppression is the crop. Suffering is the harvest. Freedom turns the soil for new ground.

Try to squeeze air in your fist and you are left with no air. This is how it is with Love, with life, with freedom. This is how fleeting freedom can be: You exhale and feel freedom fly into your soul. By the time you inhale, you have taken freedom for granted. You inhale your own bondage in your very next breath. Supremacy and inferiority are gravities against which freedom pushes with every breath.

All your life you have wanted someone to listen. Freedom has been listening to you all your life. Listen to what it has to say in return.

We are like baby birds in our earth nest, hopping toward freedom's sky. Some of us taste flight for a moment before plummeting back down. Some of us never manage to feel air beneath us, or the sensation of being aloft. And some, delirious and mocked, learn to stay in that improbable sky. Those souls have stories to share that just might stir our timid wings to come alive.

Many souls confine their idea of freedom to within the walls of ideology. Freedom can live in those spaces. But it gains multitude out on the boundless savanna of Creation among its territories of Grace. It thrives in a land beyond ideas. It grows in Glory.

Freedom and oppression both exude themselves in predictable indicators. People embracing their natural features and traits is a clear sign of freedom. People rejecting, distorting, and hiding their natural features and traits is a clear sign of oppression.

Children want the freedom adults have. Adults want the freedom children have. Want the freedom *you* have. If you want it, since you already have it, you will be actively free.

Freedom requires continuous revolution. When a condition emerges and goes untreated, it calcifies. We become calcified in that condition. Keep turning your rock to water. Your water to air. Without deep, daily inner work, we flounder between caged, cage, cager. And then there is freedom. A rare air worth the effort to breathe. Get your inner oxygen as you labor.

Everything.
If you ask what freedom is worth,
the answer is, Everything.

Freedom is a kind of desert. Its harsh conditions will extract your water, will, energy, endurance. But if you adapt to its climate, and maintain your will to live there, it can purify your soul and touch your generations with medicine.

Our true freedom is from the homelessness of wandering outside of union with all things. All you have ever yearned for is but a yearning for one thing: *freedom*. You may ask how often you must free yourself. Always. You are a grain of sand at the maw of oppression's ocean. Free yourself with every breath.

At first, your ideas about life set you out exploring and discovering, a kind of being set free. If you decide to live inside your ideas and never leave them, they calcify, become tumors of fear. They enslave you. Keep your ideas wet with your tears. Keep feeling them deeply, so you can look into their shimmering pools and still see your true self clearly. Your true self is not a self. It is a communion of all living things. All your relations. Your true self is the face of life. Which is always greater and more beautiful than any idea.

The nature of the universe plays itself out inside the human soul. In the oneness of things. Perceived separation and the forgetting it births. All the storms of chaos and entropy. All the harmony and healing of union. All your teachers, all your lessons, all your classrooms, all your exams are inside you.

Sun browns the skin, marks it with evidence of the Love they have made. Freedom does the same sweet thing to your salient soul. Do not be afraid to go out into freedom's light, strip naked of your conditioning, and freedom bathe.

Laws and policies cannot grant freedom. Leaders and nations cannot grant freedom. Institutions and programs cannot grant freedom. Material wealth and social status cannot grant freedom. Titles and accolades, popularity and notoriety, none of these can grant freedom. Only you can grant yourself freedom. Only your kind can grant yourselves freedom. Freedom is your innate characteristic. To be free is to activate and populate the light that is your soul.

Freedom is like a river. You cannot touch that water and say, *Now I know freedom*. That water has already moved on, blended and merged with other water and elements, picked up sediment and sun. It has changed. To stay free, do more than touch freedom's water. Submerge yourself all the way into the river. Let the river enter you. Let your composition dissolve in the river. Become the river and its water nature and language, and you can stay free.

Water changes form to preserve its essence.
Change your ways to preserve your soul.

Observe how water teaches freedom. Against one oppression it turns to ice. Against another it turns to steam. It does what it must to retain its true self. It always finds its way back home. And remains a source for life. Those things most beautiful to us are free. And yet we so often refuse to grant ourselves this same beautiful condition.

If life does not spring from your spirit, words, or ways, how can we say you are free? And if everywhere you are, beauty blooms like the Love blush after snowmelt, surely freedom has had its way with you.

Freedom is not a thing many souls are able to see clearly. They struggle to know: *What does freedom look like?* If you want to help guide and nourish people to freedom, help them see it clearly. Paint freedom's portrait. Paint it continuously.

Freedom is a mountain that taunts you. You ache yourself up its slopes. When at last you first set your foot on the peak, new, higher peaks emerge. You look up, daunted. You feel you may never get there. In this doubt is the source of your resolve. In your memory, assemble all the doubt you have ever felt and ask it what it has done for your life. Listen closely to the answer. It will give you energy for the peaks ahead.

Freedom is not in the social groups you join, the education you achieve, knowledge you obtain. Freedom is not in your location, destination, occupation, vocation, neighborhood, nation, culture, clan, politic, program, opinions, values, house, marriage, school, clothes, style, relationships. Freedom is beautiful because it is not promised in any of these worldly things. Freedom is the rarest of gems, mined exclusively and mystically from the soul. *From the soul.*

A turtle hatchling struggled in the rising sun to reach the ocean that would save its life. Over and over it strained against sand, then water to achieve the depth that would sweep it to sea and home. Over and over, just as the hatchling felt close to realizing its yearning, the tide surged, pushing the hatchling back up high on the binding shore. The hatchling grew tired, depleted, discouraged, scared, painfully alone. Predators loomed overhead and nearby, sensing a meal. Something stubborn in the hatchling, a kind of force, would not let the hatchling give up. With a final outburst of energy and action, the hatchling breached the tide surge, felt the relaxed expansion of ocean, swam out into its boundless release. This story, dear soul, is freedom.

What does freedom feel like? All your life you have been swimming inside a single raindrop on a rock in the desert. One day, you decide you want more. You dare to leave the raindrop. You endure the fear of leaving. You endure the leaving. You leave. Your old dream ends. You wake into wonder and wind. You are swimming now in a pure water ocean with no shores. You drown there. Not into death. Into life. Freedom fills the lungs of your soul with a divine air and drowns you to life. Freedom breathes.

Freedom is not a destination. You never arrive permanently. Freedom is an atmosphere with endless realms. Break through into one, and a higher one appears beyond that. We are never forever free, only forever opening into freedom. This is more than enough. This is everything.

If you say, *I have achieved freedom*, this is like saying, *I have achieved the best physical condition of my life.* Satisfied and content, you feel you can afford to stop exercising and minding your diet. By the next morning, after you skipped your workout and ate half a cake, your condition has already declined. Fitness is fleeting without continuous devotion. Freedom also works this way.

Freedom is not partial, not conditional. It is not a mist that condenses along group boundaries and borders. Freedom is an air that destroys and devours boundaries. If you try to bottle freedom for your people exclusively, you lose freedom entirely in the end. Freedom fire dies in selfish atmospheres. Kill your prejudices if you want freedom. Let your heart explode into all living things.

If you don't feel free, you aren't free. Freedom is an undeniable sensation. An overwhelming exhalation. It recognizes itself. If you experience its brave blessings, you will know.

FEAR AND FREEDOM

It is necessary to find and touch the root of this fear that births supremacy-inferiority virus. Existential anxiety is the root. For some, the climate or environment with which their ancestors contended created a chronic anxiety their descendants have inherited. For others, some grave group trauma reverberated down the generations. Some, beyond their ancestral endowment, experience wounding in their own lifetime that births deep anxiety about existing. The endpoint of this anxious, cumulative despair is a wide-open vulnerability to supremacy and inferiority.

For many, a continuous cry comes from their spirit: *I am terrified of this existence. I am not even sure I exist. At any moment I could disappear. Or the sky could fall on me.* Such souls may seek to quell their panic by exerting control over the world. Or by pleading for the world to control them.

The one most likely to be your oppressor is you. If you care to be truly free, fill your life with countless daily rebellions. Self-oppression comes in waves of blatant fear and creeping tides of insecurity. If you do not swim for the shore of your own truth and freedom, oppression current will take you out to sea and drown you. Stay centered in yourself so you can be aware of your condition.

Overthrow your fears.
The only revolution that matters.

Do not doubt that many will run from freedom. Panicked as though they are running from death. Show them true death. The un-life they are living. The end doom to which they are running. Show them not through shame, guilt, scolding.

Show them the urgency of Love. The vital mirror that shows us, through contrast, the fear we choose as our conqueror and the rewards we reap when we go unconquered.

As you begin to approach freedom, the unfamiliarity and sacrifices it demands can make slavery feel more desirable. Many slaves turn back at this point. They grow nostalgic about the plantation, the reservation, falling into denial about their long suffering. At this point, it takes determined souls to urge and nurture their people the rest of the way into freedom.

Fear is a code talker. You hear it saying one thing. Its true message is something else. Learn to decipher its confusion and you can speak to it in a language that calms its panicked flame.

Change the conditions that create fear and you cure the condition that creates supremacy-inferiority. Fear is that condition. The fallow ground from which suffering grows.

She let her soul roam beyond all the external boundaries she had been taught. She undomesticated into peace.

You may have inherited your ancestors' fear of uprising against oppression. You may have also inherited their courage. Two streams running through your choices, your way of life. What a blessing: You get to choose.

Some will never make even a squeak about freedom, so terrified are they to become visible among the herd. Your visibility will be one of your offerings to your people and humanity. What comes with that is for you to face, and worthy of your sacrifice. For a soul like yours, invisibility in the face of oppression is a far crueler fate.

Fear can start as an abrasion on the skin.
Catch it before it becomes an infection in your bones.

So many of us, like the slaves of old, so greatly fear angering or disappointing the master (society itself), that we betray our own spirits. Spirits that by their very nature pulse in the direction of life, which is a spirit, too. The spirit of freedom. Bound up things decipher cages as birdless wings. They want to fly, but instead of being a bird, would rather the cruel comfort that bondage brings.

Build an aura of Loving protection around those souls willing to do this freedom work. For they will be assaulted as though by a sky of arrows. But the glory of their labor will live on in the ease of your children. And in the dire healing of a tired land. Many people are strong enough to run downhill. Who will run uphill with you? In those souls you will find your revolution.

Oppression is a bullying spirit. At the heart of all bullies is fear. You will not convince fear to dissolve itself inside a bully. Dissolve yourself into Spirit in the presence of fear.

Fear is a prison.
Don't be your own warden.

Everybody is scared. You aren't afflicted. You're alive. When you step outside, you feel air on your face. This is freedom. When you are alive, you feel fear in your body. This too is freedom. The sensation of possibility. Yes, things could go wrong. But what if they go right? What then? Are you afraid? Congratulations. You are alive. Beautiful things are still possible. You are one of them.

An animal caught in a trap will gnaw off its limbs to get free. A human caught in bondage will gnaw off its soul to remain in bondage. Many humans prefer suffering to change. Fear is our master even as we claim to worship the Divine, which is a force of freedom. The personal rules we create to protect our wounds can imprison us. We can be caught in a snare, but lash out violently at the hand of Grace that arrives to help set us free. Some of the people most aggressively against your revolution are not truly rejecting your revolution, they are fleeing their fear. Nurture them through this veil and they can become genuine champions of the revolution. Fear magnifies pain. Love reassures pain that it is in good hands. Pain, a needful newborn, calms down. You know what to do.

Being a revolutionary is not a question of risking death. All things are dying even as they live. The worst dying of all is slavery. Being a revolutionary is a question of living. How do you choose to live? Whose dreams are you fulfilling? Dreams of your oppressors who despise you, or your ancestors who Love you? Risk being alive. Your purpose passes through your greatest fears to manifest in the world. Your fears literally birth your freedom.

Breathe deeply.
You've always made it through.

The most effective way to jump in the water is to jump in the water. Whatever it is you are afraid to begin, to try, to dare, to release, the most effective way is to begin. This may seem obvious, but so often we stand at the edge of the water trying to come up with the perfect strategy for jumping in the water. We can spend years standing there, waiting to feel ready. This tendency is likely rooted in fear, anxiety, and insecurity, which we respond to by telling ourselves we need a better plan. We need to know how to start. We need to be more qualified. This is a control delusion. We start by letting go of control and self-judgement long enough to take the plunge, to feel ourselves in free fall, to feel the fright of not holding on to anything. It is a moment of faith that we experience over and over until we become more comfortable with the sensation of leaping. This is the only way to jump in the water. By jumping. You could spend your life preparing to begin. Or you could spend your life beginning, over and over. Each time blessing your freedom ways.

If you are afraid to shine your true light, afraid of how people will react, consider this: You are an actual sun on earth. And everyone is lost in the dark and freezing. Whatever you are is singular. Your singularity makes you a sun. A source of life. Bear the discomfort of standing out. Stand out. Peace will grow in. And you will bless life on earth as you rise, swoon, and set.

She gathered sage in springtime.
And her courage all through the year.

Nurture yourself through fret of dying. This fear has killed and suffocated more revolutions than can be conceived. Dying releases your revolution spirit into a limitless form that travels and endures. To exist outside of revolution is another kind of dying. It is not a living. Everything is dying. Your choice of living brings meaning and purpose to this infinite circle of coming and going, of forever being in the currents of change.

Numbing, perceived comfort and security are among the most powerful tools of oppression. Oppressed people can grow so familiar with and used to their condition, they experience a tragic kind of comfort. An emotional attachment to their condition. When someone proposes freedom, they will lash out at that person for threatening their ingrained dependence on comfort. If slaves are comfortable enough, they will fasten their own shackles each day, even if a terrible suffering lives inside their peculiar comfort.

Slaves given a shack to live in, rags to wear, and slop to eat will eventually believe they are being treated well as long as the master is not lashing them. Comfort and security are perceived and relative. If you want freedom, eventually you have to give up your token comfort and believe you are worthy of a better life. Freedom will cost you your slave attachments. You will have to surrender your slave amenities.

An elephant trained into submission through increasingly smaller chains, and then ropes, is ultimately held in place by a tiny thread. It forgets its power. Oppressed people are beautiful wild horses standing in a pen. The gate is open, but they are afraid to run to their true emancipation. Escaping the psychological chains of slavery takes psychological examination of harm and maladaptive response. And continuous rendering of what wellness and wholeness look like in mundane life. Stay acquainted with open pastures.

Unshackle yourself from fear of your oppressor's reaction to how you act, speak, dress, walk, talk, wear your hair, feel, gather, celebrate, mourn, build, create, move, groove, remember, sing, dance, work, parent, cook, eat, pray, heal, relate, exist. Spend the rest of your life breaking this appeasement chain. Your oppressor is not your god. Look higher for that affirmation.

Slaves, whip-scarred and tremulous, are nervous to approach the boundaries of action or vitality circumscribed by society. Slaves fear the lash. Anticipate it. Are much more comfortable and familiar with avoiding the boundary. Staying in place. Even if that place is a place of disintegration. Even if that place churns their children into institutional systems that carry them away from family, community, and self on rafts of despair, down rivers of false hope, into fetid deltas of isolation and dying internal light.

To make it plain, as the old folks say, slaves often are afraid to become well again. To endure the long journey back across years of abbreviated existence, back to the place of wellness, to retrieve its essence and transport it through the desert of time and forgetting, to this now-ness of days. This fear forebodes slaves into paralysis, disbelieving in their right to thrive. They disconnect from thoughts and actions that lead to vitality. They are afraid to act as a group to heal the group. Slaves recoil at the idea of abundance, of having their own land. The only property they are willing to acquire is suffering. Unless slaves find a way together to be brave. Indeed, slaves have found those ways.

To one whose whole life has been bathed in supremacist affirmation, questioning this supremacy feels like death. Certain oblivion. Suddenly, such a soul feels the biting cold of disaffirmation, and wonders how the world could be so cruel. In this moment, the person is a danger to self and the world. A soul swamped with viral supremacy believes it is being persecuted when others rise into their freedom. Like a sandcastle at the shore believing the ocean tide is unjust, that its manufactured sand structure should last forever.

Those who perpetuate genocide, and their offspring who live on the entrails of genocide, fear nothing more than that genocide will be perpetrated on them. The moment you begin thinking of dominating others, you birth an eternal fear that those others will one day dominate you.

If you demand that your kindred revolutionaries and people hew to every grain of your personal revolution values, you will lose them. This is your revolution no more than it is their revolution, no matter the shine, shade, credit, or criticism placed on you. This is true especially for your particular freedom language. All revolutions suffer semantic discord and erosion, people arguing over the validity of certain words and labels. Stay humble, open, and compassionate together as you attune to the meaning of your freedom words. Meaning is a river, not a stone. It changes continuously as historical experience manifests in every moment. Garden your language together daily. It holds, purifies, and feeds your stories. Which hold, purify, and feed your revolution.

If you ask people to entirely change their way of life, they may revolt against your request. You will have already lost them. This is how fearful and aversive many people are to change. This does not mean you should not advocate for entire change. Only that your revolution benefits from being aware of the human condition regarding change. People are much more open to the idea of gradual adjustment to their way of life. This allows them a gradual adjustment to their self-ideas. Self-ideas can turn on your revolution. In a flash, self-ideas can go from a prideful source of common cause, to a chosen cage of rejection incarcerating people away from change.

The eternals have understood forever how human beings are when it comes to change. These truths are not new lessons recently discovered by the science of your oppressors, as they would have you believe. People are more likely to dilate into change under certain conditions. Superordinate goals. Clear vision and values. Clear, common language. Clear direction and purpose. Clear destination. Consistent messaging. Timely rewards and gratification. Clear personal and group benefits. Equal personal and intergroup power within the change initiative. Sincere, group-devoted, inspiring leadership. Learn the recipe that opens to change the flower that is the human mind. This recipe is available everywhere. In people who are changing. Solicit their story. Gather and share these stories. Bring the inner journeys out into the circle and hold them to the fire of your people gathered in Love.

Humans recreate what we know. Even as we are trying to escape what we know. This is why revolutions often literally progress in circles. No need to fight against the circle. Ride the river. Use its natural current. Freedom work is more about letting go than it is about building anew. Until we release our old ways, we strain to build new ways. Do not calendar change. Change the calendar that fear decides.

Be willing to be imprisoned in bars, walls, and infamy as retribution for your freedom work, so you may end your long, terrible imprisonment of the soul. Have your people hold hands and approach the river of fear together. If you face the river collectively, you can see it is a water whose depth and current can be overcome and crossed into sovereign land.

Caste systems are held together by the scar tissue of fear and pain. Adhesions only dissolved by potency of Love for oneself, one's people, and for life. To cure this caste condition, treat the fear and pain. Speak of it directly, explicitly. Name it. Purge it in ceremony and ritual. Do not lose yourself in escapist public attention to fickle surface arguments and ideas that come and go easier than breeze.

When you and your people reach the river you will cross and follow to the Promised Land, some will have not yet overcome their fear. They will turn back. Love them and keep going. Some—the coming change made real by the sound and sight of water—will struggle, resist, even panic and attack you. Love them and keep going. Some will take your hand and wade with you through the water. Love them and keep going. All your senses will be peaked. The moment may feel like a dream. An impossible happening. Stay awake and keep going. Now you are in freedom's light. It will guide you the rest of the Glory way.

When you work toward freedom, you threaten to change people's way of life. Many of them will resist you as though you are killing their god. For many, their way of life is their god. Be a beacon of light in the face of their panic. Help them recognize their idolatry. You cannot determine for them their god. Point them to their own soul. Their soul will show them who their true god is. As they find their own sacred way, they will be more open to changing their way of life. You won't be their deliverance. That will be their own weaving of sweetgrass and sage.

TARGET THE VIRAL ENERGY

Be clear as to who your oppressor is. Oppression is a virus, a spirit potential that lives in every soul. Some let this spirit grow in them. Others actively cultivate it. Some devote themselves to healing their entire lives of this virus. You can learn to see the difference. As you learn, give yourself permission to build with your kindred people and to reject the lash and plans of your oppressor. See freedom clearly and you can remain in freedom lands.

Genotype-focused warfare has been killing humanity for millennia. It is a warfare of appearances and social categories. We need soul seers capable of gazing beneath easy surface appearances and recognizing rivers of wellness and sickness in the soul. We must learn in our time to engage not in genetic warfare, but in kinetic welfare. Welfare against sickness in the energy streams of spirit, thought, idea, mind, and mentality. Welfare against the places where these energies reside: body, language, culture, and systems. We need energy work.

People will not support your revolution just because they look like you or are of your oppressed kind. Some of these people will be your fiercest opponents, because your revolution threatens their way and idea of life and of themselves. It scares them to death. Do not pour your revolution resources and attention according to social category. Pour according to who is devoted to your revolution. You will know these people by the moments in which they take their stand.

The true enemy of any people is not any other people as a whole, but the attitudes and energies within those cultural groups. Basing freedom work in opposition to a category of people allows the true viral threat to escape untouched, as it slithers between the highly permeable walls that separate our social categories. Supremacy virus is an airborne, thought borne, spirit borne contagion. It recognizes no boundaries.

Your revolution is kinetic, not genetic. It is not against an innate group. It is against a spirit, an energy in the form of ideas, attitudes, systems, cultures, ways of life. If you target a group, you miss the parasite, which slithers between hosts as easily as air, and respects no group boundaries. Its prey is not a social category. Its prey is the human organism and its reproductive ways. Attack people's social category and you miss the target that is viral supremacy. Your message loses steam, power, and validity out through the window of your generalization.

It is against the nature of many souls to join in a revolution that is based on absolute declarations about groups of people. Generalizing assault appeals less to souls the more entrenched they are in their own sacred Love for self and life. If you want to recruit healthy souls to your freedom work, your social concepts must be healthy. Your definition of the cause, and of other human beings, needs integrity and sanctity. You cannot wage a sacred work using desecrating language, ideas, and paradigms.

Within a group of one million people exist one million souls. One million unique spirits, personalities, and personal life journeys. It is difficult to rally masses to engage in freedom work against a category of people as enemy. Boundaries are far too blurred. Too many of those we seek to rally would experience an internal dissonance or conflict. Human variance is as much a truth as is the variance within all of life. Even ominous cultural legacies cannot erase this truth. Choose your target wisely.

Masses will not follow a course of revolution when they are not potently convinced they would be in fact working against the true threat. This cloudiness unsettles those with at least a moderate sense of compassion and respect for humanity at large, and those who are not flagrantly engulfed in the hissing of hateful rage.

Global conflict is not intrinsic to the physical and cultural makeup of groups. Conflict is essentially an energetic storm we inherit from those before us. Effective social systems are functionally competent in this language of energetic interplay. The call is to create healing systems that conduct the symphony of soul.

THE FAVORING OF THINGS

Supremacy societies create two caste tiers: *favored and unfavored*. Those who are favored, considered part of the supreme kind, inherit privilege, protection, access, and heroic regard. And those who are unfavored, considered inferior to the favored ones, inherit the hard crust of a life of unceasing assault on their existence. Favored and unfavored can exist in the same family, even in the same person. Spouses and partners often catch a social ride on the backs of their Lovers who are favored. Favoring is a matter of identifiable and secret traits. An imagined conclusion. Who the world says you are.

One who lives swaddled with favor at the center of an unnatural circle is the last one to see, admit, reckon with the favoring. These souls live in such a state of insecurity that any attempt to point out the unjust favoring creates a sense of persecution. A sense of being marginalized even without having any real experience of what it feels like to live chronically in a hostile, multi-generational margin.

Favored people learn to develop a pledge of allegiance to not seeing the oppression their kind perpetuates. A code of nonparticipation even as they participate. Claiming not to see the very trait by which their entire existence is defined, protected, and exalted is their guilt suppression mechanism. Their denial mantra. Their way to continue existing in nonexistence. But their denial makes them a slave master. An oppressor of souls. Their only way out of their inferno of guilt and inner conflict is to acknowledge the group sickness of which they are a part. To say, *Yes, this thing is real. It lives and breathes and kills. My life is built upon terror. These lands are a killing ground. I have received and choose to receive favor atop this mountain of bones.*

The more favored that people are along one or more social dimensions, the more self-centered they may be. It does not occur to them that their favoring is based on a prejudice of supremacy. They assume they are favored because they are favorable. This deduced idea of themselves makes them harmful in the social realm of living things. The more unfavored people are, the more self-centered they may also be. Suffering draws them into themselves, narrows their field of vision. Plunged into survival mode, their attentive energy is consumed in chronic crisis condition. They are an emergency.

Suppressed guilt and shame in the favored kind creates a profound constipation of the soul. Spirit cannot flow out or in naturally. To try to compensate, the favored kind resort to seeking to control everything, especially in others. Emotions, behaviors, thoughts, memories, freedom.

Favored people often disdain recognizing their own favor. Often cannot bear to look inside and acknowledge their supremacy virus, the legacy they inhabit and uphold. They are pained to see the world in terms of the very differences by which they live, by which society ascribes who is more human. If you point out their infected way of seeing and thinking, they abort the moment. For in that moment their lifelong sense of their own goodness is in jeopardy.

The most dangerous citizens are those who deny and suppress their supremacy sickness. They believe they are champions of the decency brigade. But because everything they touch is stained with supremacy, their efforts to be a part of the revolution are fated to abet the regression. Avoid letting them mix into your crowd and disappear. They will do so much harm in their anonymity.

People of favored cultures do not see themselves as cultures at all. They see themselves as above culture, an exemplar of what it means to be individual human excellence. All others are viewed as groups of cultural creatures, exotic, mysterious, primal. This is how oppressors build their righteous case for domination.

People often defer to the supremacy sickness present in their social relations, even over their own morality and values. Their relationships are more important to them, even if those people are poisoning them with false ideas about others. This is how the faithful kinship of neutral souls becomes an enabling hiding place for supremacy and oppression. Prejudice stains the soul the way dye stains a bone, down to the marrow.

The larger and more powerful your body grows, the more sensitive you should be to how your presence affects others. The more powerful your social favoring grows, the more sensitive you need to be to how your favoring impacts unfavored people and influences other favored people. Take care not to bruise the world.

You may find yourself wondering about the favored kind: *BeLoved, why are you incompetent, illiterate, without fluency in the souls of the oppressed? Why are you unable to coexist with living things?* That is the question. Do not offer to be their teacher. Invite them to learn from the teacher that is their own soul.

It is hard to find humility in the web of humanity when your society oozes the message of your superiority through its every pore and vein. But it is possible, if your soul yearns enough to heal its infection and find peace among living things. It is hard to dissolve your guilt, to admit your poisoned ideas of other groups, to breach the veil of your fear, to see clearly the sacredness you have been taught to denounce, to reap the anger and hurt of the unfavored masses, to confront other favored ones for their sickness. It is painfully hard to be socially favored, saturated in supremacy, and live in a natural world that contradicts your life of lies. Still, this pain does not compare to the pain such a soul causes the world. Upon this energetic scale, the world decides itself.

Those who exist in a highly analytic manner void of soul, sensitivity, feeling, compassion, often do so because they are comfortable and secure inside of thinking. They believe it affords them a measure of control. Living in harmony with living things requires humility, surrender, and an openness of heart and spirit. A bowing to the wilderness of living things.

The further your orbit is from the illegitimate sun of being the favored kind, the colder, harsher your atmosphere inside the galaxy of the favored ones. Displace your oppressor from your orbital center. Manifest your own galaxy. Make your own sun.

Just because society has worked for you and yours as a favored kind, doesn't mean it isn't oppressing others. Your satisfaction does not determine whether the culture is just.

The most frequent recipients and beneficiaries of welfare and entitlement programs are those people who are favored presently, historically, and generationally by society's supremacy sicknesses. They cannot stand to think of these benefits as unjust, so they spend their lives weaving inner stories about their right to these benefits. For them, only their supremacy can explain how they receive what others do not. When you consider enlightening the mind and perspective of such a soul, know you are facing not just a person, but also a tightly woven story made of millions of repeating threads. You are seeking to untangle a web of millions of favored souls repeating these threads to each other. They are a collective hum reassuring each other: *We deserve what we have. We deserve what we have. We deserve what we have. And they who do not have it, must not deserve it. Isn't it so?*

Privilege, by its very nature, is an uninterrupted stream of affirmation. Consider what this stream does to the generational confidence and assertion of those who swim in this stream. Consider the generational impact on those who live in the absence of this stream. When assessing what various groups achieve, how they live, their relative wellness and abundance, consider this stream of daily, lifelong, generational affirmation. It will help cure your false ideas.

It is a privilege to breathe. If you care to benefit humanity and living things, instead of claiming you are not privileged, examine your privilege, the harm it causes, and the opportunities it provides you to serve the greater good. Become privilege-informed and intimate.

You can work hard in your life and still be privileged and entitled. Privilege and entitlement have nothing to do with hard work and everything to do with an absence of barriers and hostility, and the presence of social and systemic favor. Your character is not at issue. Your place in the caste system, and the place of others, is.

Privilege is an addiction. An intoxication. People will not surrender it without dire personal cause. In their minds, the end of their privilege is the beginning of their poverty and unjust treatment. In truth, the end of oppression is the end of privilege. People will fight against the end of oppression simply because it will mean the end of their privilege. This terrifies them.

As you move into favored spaces, ensure that you favor your socially unfavored self. You will be pressured to become the image of the favored ones and to abandon who you are. Pressured to fit into your assigned role of being a tolerated presence. Pressured to be a more acceptable version of your kindred and unfavored people. When you are isolated in these spaces, is vital that you actively favor yourself. This isn't just best practice. It is survival.

Extreme favoring and unfavoring are both threats to public safety, public health, and public prosperity. They are two ends of a spectrum given life by the original virus of existential fear. Favored and unfavored people are bound together in a pulsing, tumorous entanglement strangling the life from each. Focus your revolution on dissolving favoring and you dissolve unfavoring with it. Tend to the roots that make people so attracted to favoring and unfavoring in the first place. Cure the condition of fear and insecurity, and its hosts: social and soulful isolation. Cure the climate and ways of being that are adapted to this oppression atmosphere. This is a public crisis, not an agenda for special interest groups. This is a moment of fate for living things.

In a society of supremacy and oppression, many wake in the morning abruptly, anxiously, roughly. Oppressed people are cast back into the nightmare of being under assault. Oppressors are cast back into the nightmare fear of having their supremacy lie and system destroyed. Oppressors are obsessed with being overthrown, which happens when you sit on an unnatural, invalid, unsustainable throne. In free societies, indigenous in relational wealth, people wake up gradually, peacefully, gently. They move according to spirit into their day. The objective is not surviving genocide or hoarding materials, status, or power. There is no objective. Only dilation into purpose as dictated by what the soul says on this day.

How would you feel about yourself if you were stripped of all your titles, status, and social power? That feeling is the ground where your true work begins, dear soul. Deep inside the unfavored reality of your existence.

Favored ones are cursed by the favoring.

You will know the descendants of slave masters and favored people by their peculiar tension and energy. They can be stiff and closed and uncomfortable with soulfulness and verve. For in the soul are wild doings and reckonings to be had.

What is social power? It is the power to affect social reality. All persons possess social power. Some are more endowed by society and systems to exert their social power. Exerting it to oppress others turns this power into a poison. Using it to liberate turns this power into paradise. Social power is the mechanism, the channel by which supremacy attitudes may be exercised. Social power and supremacy attitudes are not one and the same. Each can travel separately. Manifest independently. Social power is a function of society, but attitudes are a mental function of the obedient heart.

Social power is a force as small and sweetened as a smile, as conspicuous and soured as the brio of war. Social power exercised against the collective good and in disharmony with Creation is not true power at all. It is spiritual impotence. It is a desperate bluster shuddering at its own vacancy. Social power spilled in the direction of Life blesses the larger self that is the world and fills the cup of soul satisfaction. When we pour out our goodness we reenact Creation and its creating impulse. A chorus of effusive sighs releases, a basket is woven of our giftedness, of our vital energy: that which gives life. From this basket all living things may plunder for their enrichment. This offering of our elemental produce to the human and living marketplace taps our spiritual orchard into Creation omnipotence. The fruit we then grow is not from the strange tree of social power. It is manna and magnificence bursting ripe and ready from each moment of modest, mundane servitude. So that beauty may be deciphered from suffering, goodness forged from temptation's easy soil. And a rain called to sweeten our crop of moments.

Do not say you cannot be supremacist and oppressive in the way your oppressor is because your oppressor holds all the power. Social power is fickle over time and condition. If social power is the only thing keeping you from being an oppressor, you are already an oppressor in waiting. Waiting for the winds to shift in the direction of your oppression empowerment. Tend to your soul, to your spirit. Hold on to your sacred essence. Then, if your kind finds yourselves with a new kind of social power, that of a potential oppressor, your inner condition will prevent you from being a monster on earth.

Power movements of oppressed people seek to attain the end of suffering. Power movements of oppressors seek to maintain socially sanctioned superiority. These two power notions are distinct species. When advocates of the caste status quo proclaim they are simply protecting their peoples' place in society, the place they seek to protect was never their rightful place to begin with. It was a dehumanizing, monstrosity of a place from the first moment it took on light in the poisoned embers of someone's mind. Do not fall for this equating of power. One power is a sacredness asserting itself. The other is a sickness protecting its infection campaign.

The power to destroy the world lives in you. You cannot say you, or your people, do not have power. The most oppressed can carry an intensified, concentrated power, that when loosened through the cracks of opportunity, rampage into the world as a plague of rage and resentment, of vengeance and wrath. Embrace the truth of this power, that you may never abuse it.

Social power does not exist only as an absolute. It exists in varying degrees within souls, throughout institutions, and across time and situations. If you can kill one life, you can kill all life. If you can heal one life, you can heal all life. You are not just a microcosm of the universe. You are the universe in all its macro potential.

Do not doubt your medicine.
The Love force in you alone can heal the world.

If you believe your people, no matter how oppressed, have no power, you have yourself erased their humanity, their history, their legacy, their spirit in the world. Watch your words and beliefs closely. They are wild things. They take you places.

The question is: *If you had the opportunity to oppress your oppressor, would you?* What is your honest truth? Here, in your answer, is where the work begins.

The descendants of the favored kind inherit a hell the roots of which they are unlikely to realize. Often, they possess little of the spirit openness and humility necessary to exist in harmony with humanity. They feel a painful marginalization, a prison of energetic guilt and shame they too often transmute into anger, rage, and disdain for unfavored people.

The gravitational force of generational supremacy sickness is powerful. So much so that all intentions by oppressed people toward freedom drift toward a central orbit: comforting and pleasing those who are favored. Our freedom language loses its truth, becomes watered down to appease favored ones. We fear calling the sickness what it is. No one wants to touch off the profound rage and wrath of favored people. Favored people know this. They are raised to employ defenses against any direct naming of their offense against humanity. They weaponize their guilt. It becomes the subterranean current moving through all souls and social expression. An oppressor trauma so tender and painful no one is allowed to trigger it. Maintenance of oppressor comfort reigns more important than the freedom of those they oppress. This is the graveyard where revolutions go to die.

Living as a beneficiary of supremacy creates a lifelong dependence on existential comfort. An inability to endure discomfort in how one is seen or sees the self. Comfort is the crown and the castle of supremacy. The *superior* ones wear comfort as a crown indicating their reign and royalty.

They live in the cold, soulless castle of chronic comfort, with high stone walls and deep toxic moats separating themselves from the peasant masses, from the reality of the true world outside their cultivated enclave of supreme social order. Comfort keeps them at a distance from the terrible idea that maybe they are not entirely good people. Comfort keeps their self-idea in good standing. It takes pathological daily justification of their personal way of life inside a supremacy society to remain in comfort. Therefore, comfort is an unholy grail for the favored ones.

It is precisely at the point at which the turning social tide begins to feel to favored people like persecution that those who would be free must push forward. The last incline to the mountain peak is fraught with high winds, thin air, a barrenness of shelter, and the hammering glare of an unrepentant sun. Many who started this climb lose their will here, the summit so close. Their strained minds and spirits start to ponder the way back down. Who is willing to endure this discomforting tectonic shift in social favoring? This is a revolution question. What rare soul is able to live at freedom's peak?

·

THE RECKONING

When a ripe freedom reckoning begins its slow burn in supremacy societies, favored people fear being honest about their natural impulses and affinities toward other favored people. Dishonesty results, accompanied by an endless array of contortions, rationalizations, denials, and masquerades. What ails favored people is not their natural attraction to their favored kind, but the unhealed condition in them that makes more exclusive, absolute, and rigid their preferences.

A society that does not reckon with its inhumanity reaps only more inhumanity. No matter how many laws it passes or how it dresses its story in flattering ways. The propaganda a society uses to deny and flee its sickness further becomes that sickness. Words become poison. Acts become fraudulence. Culture becomes a cesspool fertile for the growth of only that particular sickness. Life in such a place becomes not life, but a daily sweeping current moving in the direction of fulfillment for that virus: *death*. Reckoning will happen, and it will hurt worse than almost anything, but it will yield life. Or reckoning will not happen, and it will hurt worse than anything and yield death.

The meek shall inherit the earth not because they are weak. They are not weak. They are meek in that they are humble. They are submitted to the unavoidable oneness of nature. The meek shall inherit the earth because those sick with supremacy are on a terminal path of destruction. Self-destruction. No matter how many fortresses they build, they cannot stop the tide of freedom. The only way to survive freedom is to become freedom. Many cannot. They have sold their soul to fear. For them, winter is coming. Winter is always coming.

Oppressors and those whose kindred kind have benefitted from oppression and supremacy require intensive, ongoing retreat and repair of their idea of themselves. Atonement, eradication of denial, acceptance of cultural culpabilities and injustices. No way exists around this pain. The path is through the pain. On the other side, relief at last from generations of guilt, self-mutilation, and suffering.

Many whose kind have been oppressed are loathe to admit their potential to be an oppressor. Yet their oppression wounds have carved out a niche in their soul for oppressor spirit to fill. They have been made ready by their suffering. The transposition is an easy one. Arrogance says, *I cannot be*

79

an oppressor. My people have been long oppressed. Enlightenment says, If oppressor spirit exists in any soul it can exist in all souls. I will keep my wary watch.

Pain can make people self-consumed. Self-centered. Insensitive to others. This is true of oppressors and oppressed. The pain of an oppressor is a pain of the soul's unremitting guilt. Of a serrating conflict with life's relational nature. It is a pain of denial and suppression. A haunting need to justify, dehumanize, and further oppress. The pain of the oppressed is a pain of separation from the wholeness of the essential soul. A pain of drifting light, of rescinded hope. Both pains roast in fear and wail in denial. Both pains are willing to become peace, if only they are duly watered with the truth of Sacredness.

HEAL THE SUPREMACY-INFERIORITY VIRUS

Now is the time in our human journey to heal to extinction the acute ailment of supremacy-inferiority, in spirit and in all its manifestations. No matter who you are, the first step is to look into yourself and say to your very soul, *I have been poisoned all my life, since my first breath. I choose now and forever to cleanse and purify myself and my life of this ill spirit. I choose to do this healing work. That I may not be a harmful presence in this world. That I may learn what it means to honor the sacredness that is all living things.*

Earth culture wisdom understands supremacy is a sick spirit residing in all people. It is we who carry it forward, perpetuate it, participate in it, ratify and validate it, permit and enable it. Each of us. In our generational bones. In the stories we tell and do not tell. In our ways of feeling, seeing, saying, being. Supremacy is a pathology that tilts life off its axis of balance. This imbalance breeds suffering and pain in every thread of soul. Supremacy is a spirit of control, power, and oppression. It is intrinsically *anti-life*. For life is freedom, liberation, self-determination. You cannot say you are a champion of life even as you destroy life on earth. You cannot uphold only the lives you say are chosen. All life is chosen. Hypocrisy maintains supremacy. If our sacred web of life is to be whole and well, we must abandon hypocrisy and achieve the courage to usher this old, tragic spirit out of this world. Supremacy will cling to the world in a death grip, sensing its demise. It will flare and plume in the season of its fatality. This is when we gather ourselves in a strength of ceremony, and with the collective breath and heartbeat of our ancestors and ones to come, sing this foul death out to its death, sing life upon life back into our earth of Grace. Now is the time for our great healing. The call is for you who chooses to be a living thing.

A moment of emotional fate occurs when you see or think about a person or people you do not know. A feeling moves through you. This feeling is the child of all your associations with visible and invisible human traits. This feeling shapes your energetic connection to those people thereafter. In this seemingly sudden but actually old feeling in you, supremacy does its work. This is where you do your healing work as well. The undoing of associations happens here, in this tide pool of feeling and idea associations. People need guidance and support in recognizing, naming, lifting, and examining their feelings and the roots involved. Your revolution is powerful because it changes the stories and structures that house the thick, lifelong, generational vines connecting foul ideas with fatal feelings. These vines are the true chains of oppression. Clear a path through this jungle.

Supremacy virus creates massive inflammation in a soul. Treat the cause of the inflammation: *the virus*. Suppressing the inflammation through avoidance, denial, and rationalization only empowers the inflammation to come roaring back even more acutely the moment conditions are fertile for the virus to dance.

If you do not take, then dissolve, the slave and slave master in you, they will tear apart your integrity as a living thing. You have everything to lose. Especially life. Heal the supremacy-inferiority virus in your soul, and you keep your generations from inheriting hell from you. If this is not motive enough to do the inner work, you are not likely to do the work at all.

When you oppress another, you inflict a terrible wound to your own soul, eroding your humanity. This wound is passed on through your generations, becoming a culture of people who struggle to exist as human with other humans. You have destroyed your soulful beauty and the offspring flowers it might have borne.

Because this virus lives in the spirit, your cure must be spiritual. Because it lives in the mind, your cure must be mindful. Because it lives in the heart, your cure must be emotional. The cure has a calling to go where it is needed.

For favored people whose souls gush with guilt, only one way out of the guilt exists. Face the virus and purge it. The guilt is a pain that grows not from being a *good person* free of prejudice and oppressive, supremacist ways. The guilt pain thrives because their soul hosts prejudice, oppression, and supremacy and they deny it. Denial is the gravity suppressing the good in their soul from rising, from condensing into an active atmosphere that would banish the viral plague. Acknowledging an infection is medicine for the cure.

All soul healing is a healing from oppression.
A freedom process.

Do not hoard your oppression virus. You have gathered it. Now let it go. Just because you carry the sickness does not mean you are the sickness. *You are a soul.* Let this infection emancipate from you. Dissolve the supremacy-inferiority sickness in you by facing your guilt and shame, which are always there, and dismissing them. Then, practice Loving yourself in a soulful way. Those soaked in soulfulness are naturally humbled out of feeling supreme and into overwhelming, grateful communion.

Supremacy cultures think and speak not according to the true interwoven nature of the world, but in dichotomies, fragments, and separations. This is the only way to remain somewhat sane while oppressing or being oppressed. The consequence is that such societies believe they are separate cultures of people, each with entirely insulated grievances. In truth, we are a collective human soul splintered by a core wound manifesting as cultures of people.

If you shun the slave or slave master spirits in you, those spirits will burrow deeper into you for defensive self-preservation, and gain strength. Sit with them. Break bread. Get to know them. Learn what they want. Where they come from. What they are afraid of. As they become ingratiated to your hospitality, they will not be so offended when you say it has grown late and ask them to leave.

Oppression may seem to benefit oppressors and their kind. But it is a way of life destined for social bankruptcy from the beginning. This is a truth for all times and inescapable. When you separate an inseparable whole into supremacy and inferiority parts, destruction is certain in all directions. Any oppression, whether passive or active, requires a spirit that sickens the oppressor. However sick those people were before they abused others, the abusing itself boosts the virus.

Sick societies tend to avoid examining their ideals. Their values morph into a cotton candy of propaganda and rhetoric. They become actors, performers, empty of the grit of soul and reckoning. Healing societies grow into a passion for collective self-examination. They develop the muscles for this freedom work.

Our responsibility to repair the world and to repair ourselves is coded into our essence. No matter how far we stray from this duty, suffering brings us back to it. When you kill what is alive, you die. When you dehumanize what is human, you die. When you oppress what is irrepressible, you die. When you divide what is indivisible, you die. When you desecrate what is sacred, you die. *You die. You die. You die.*

Supremacy mutates from dehumanization to extermination when not treated. Quarantine the virus within the host. No tolerance. Endure the cure. Incentivize healing.

Address the root cause of seeing others through the stained lens of prejudice. This kind of seeing steals the Divine from our perception and readies us to be monsters. We are all guilty of dimming the light of our collective humanity.

We fear being socially familiar with other kinds of people, because we know on the soul level that if we know them deeply, their truth will destroy our ugly idea of them. Our premature ideas will be left shamed and quivering in the cold of disaffirmation.

The worst kind of freedom workers want freedom only for their kind. This is not freedom work at all. It is deceit. Like a wolf wearing sheepskin while befriending the flock. Your oppression should make you passionate about assessing your oppression of others. Your incarceration should make you a freedom champion for everyone.

The first thing is to reject all notions that you are intrinsically inferior. You never were inferior. Kill those weeds in you every day. Each morning when you wake, determine to be free.

Silence resulting from oppression
is an incubator for social disease.
Use your freedom voice. Keep it supple.

Let it not be said of you that when they came for your neighbor around the block, you slept. When they came for your neighbor down the street, you slept. When they came for your next-door neighbor, you slept. When they came for you, you cried out for your neighbors. None came. For they were sleeping on you.

A soul that cannot bear to live in harmony and equanimity with other living things is a tortured soul. Only able to tolerate conquest and dominance. Aggrieved when not at the center of any circle. Do not grieve and guilt yourself for the slave master in you. Use that hurtful presence to instigate the fire that will free the slave in you. Let your shame burn your free soul back to life.

If you break the world down into parts, you can own, control, sell, exploit, abuse, abandon those parts. Even if those parts are human beings. This is how supremacy cultures need the world to be, a loose array of parts to serve a soulless spirit of greed. To heal what has been dehumanized and scattered from itself, be like a child intensely combing a beach, collecting shells, creating jewelry from the haul. Be a gatherer of souls. Help return beauty back to the beautiful. People moan on earth like lonely whales in the ocean, calling out for each other. Calling out for themselves. Tune yourself to this lonesome song. Be a mystic matchmaker. Bring what is lost home to itself.

When you wake up to the truth of the sacred web of life, life is solved. Collective duty makes sense. Freedom makes sense. You fill with the sensation of everything all at once, nothingness all at once, union and sovereignty all at once. This is peace.

People raise excuses from arid ground to defend emotions and attitudes that, at some deeply internal level, they are aware of as being harmful. In your freedom work, bypass all excuses and treat the virus. Treat the harm the virus leaves in its wake. Treat the soulful immune system of people and groups, that they may better resist the virus and prevent its outbreak among them.

If you sit atop a mountain long enough, you begin to feel above it all. This is also how it is with supremacy. Except a mountain grants you a humble peace. Supremacy plunges you into an arrogance of hell. You do not cure the supremacy virus in you only for the sake of others. You cure it because you are suffering. And you are worthy of peace.

Supremacy-inferiority is a virus that exists as ideas. These ideas live and breed inside of attitudes and emotions, which in turn shape and color and flavor encounters, experiences, and memories. Your work is not against groups. It is against ideas, malevolent spirits wandering the world, attracted to weakness of spirit, attracted to fear and woundedness, attracted to isolation and self-disgust. To treat the presence of these ideas in the world, treat the story wind that carries the ideas. Treat the soil of souls into which these ideas are planted as seeds. Treat the crops that rise from these ideas. Treat the farmer, the market, the distribution channels, the human demand. Treat the storytelling, the story suppressing, the story spaces. Treat everything beautiful and everything garish. Treat the ever-imaginative, single organism that is human life. Ideas infiltrate everything.

It seems everyone is trying to escape suffering by naming perpetrators and victims. But suffering breeds in the naming. Disease Loves the darkness of social blaming. Shine sunlight on fungus and it retreats and dies. Leave it to the shadows while you bicker about the forest, and fungus rejoices and expands its territory. If you want to save the castle, forget about who wears the crown, who sweeps the courtyard. Examine the water, the air. Treat the source of the sickness already coursing through the queendom. Royals and peasants both harbor the same viral culprit of their eventual death. Life has one requirement: *If you want to live, heal what is killing you.* Leave the *Us and Them* to those who aren't up to being all the way alive.

When your community is oppressed for, years, decades or centuries, it learns to exist as oppressed. This must be unlearned, and fullness of living relearned. When your community oppresses for generations, it learns to exist as an oppressor. This must be unlearned, and humility of co-existence relearned. These are the unavoidable, undeniable human realities, consequences born, crosses to bear, and bridges to be crossed.

All living things mourn what dies. Insects and animals do this as sincerely as humans. If you are sensitive enough, you can feel trees and plants aching for their fallen beLoved. As you heal into freedom, you need to mourn your former slave life, your former slave master life. If you do not mourn, you do not give honor to your passage from oppression to freedom. Freedom needs you to be honest about your attachment to your past. Mourn your many dyings, so you may live.

If you are crippled with guilt and shame about the oppressive supremacy of your kind, know that your guilt and shame are yours to carry. Yours to cure. Yours to release. Do not expect oppressed people to serve you yet again. Kill that entitlement in you. Do not punish, silence, or resent those who are oppressed to protect your guilt from being triggered. Make use of your guilt to help end oppression. Do the inner-outer work.

Hiding oppressive cultural values and ways from public critique by labeling them as *normal, standard, best practice, conventional,* or by not labeling them at all, rendering them invisible, is how supremacy parasites itself into the future. Name the virus. Name it wherever you see it, in whatever form you see it. Bring it into the light.

WELLNESS AND FREEDOM

This revolutionary life requires daily purification. Purification as each thought and feeling comes through, and each impulse arises. You will be polluted always by a social atmosphere that is allergic to the work you are doing. The way boiling oil reacts to water is the way a sickened world will react to your medicine. Purify your mind, spirit, heart, and body to withstand these violent and pervasive reactions. Notice how polluters are attracted to dumping their pollution in clean rivers. Something about the desecration, the spoiling entices them. People will want to spoil your purity. So they can then humiliate you for not being pure. You don't have to be pure. You do need to have a purification system. Remain clean enough in spirit and motive to be medicine and not malice in the meadow of this life.

In the morning, we wash our bodies clean. How often do we wash our spirits clean before the day? We feed our bodies daily. How often do we feed our spirit, soul, heart, and mind? In a materialistic culture, we value and care for the material, neglecting the immaterial. But our immeasurable nature is what we need most to preserve. For it is the atmosphere that determines the possibilities for our life.

Viruses incubate, gestate, survive, and breed in unwellness. Other people's anxiety, fear, negativity, trauma, and ill intent accumulate in us like bacteria, eventually overcoming our spirit's immune system. Spiritual hygiene is real. It can keep suffering away. Wash your spirit clean. One of the first things unwellness says is, *Change is hopeless. Nothing can be done.* Freedom work is wellness work. Reject the toxic idea that you must work yourself to death to achieve freedom. Just the opposite. Work yourself to life. You will have freedom.

The calendar does not determine your growth and healing. Your soul does. When your soul is ready, you will do the sacred work. May you be free, you precious, worthy, living thing. May you be free.

Your soul is a sacred land.
Make sure you treat it that way.

Stay in your ceremonies. Song, dance, joy, rest, release, forgiveness. Nutritional food, feelings, words, prayers, and thoughts. Communal ways. Rich solitude. Personal poetry in your ways of being. Cups of tears spilled in gratitude. Peace attitude. More kindness latitude. This, simply, is how you Love yourself, and bless your people and all living things. Send and receive Love. Receive it as though you are worthy. *You are.*

You feel sad, so your tears flow. Your flowing tears make you sad. This is how it is with freedom. Feeling Love's radiance in you, freedom flows out of you. The flow of freedom makes you feel Love. Use this sacred circle flowing in your revolution. Show us how it works.

Hold onto your joy. Dearly hold onto your joy. It is a flotation device when the waters get rough. You have every right to seek and savor joy in challenging times. Joy is best practice. Salvation mode. Chosen resistance act. Proclamation of enduring life. If you look closely, you may see reasons for joy where you did not before. Quietude and stillness have a way of shining a light on the littlest of blessings. Which are not little at all.

What is the freest thing you know?
Make that your teacher.

You can lead so many quiet revolutions today. Wear your natural hair. Show your natural face. Dress in your natural clothes. Speak your natural tongue. Pray in your natural ways. Share your natural kindness. Move in your natural rhythms. Rest and create as you are naturally inspired. Your nature holds the key to your freedom. Spring the lock.

*When someone is kind to you, make sure to plant that seed
in the soil of your worthiness. You deserve it.*

We struggle with feeling worthy partly because we forget the countless times we have been treated as worthy. Instead we remember all the times we have been mistreated, devalued, and dehumanized. This is especially true for marginalized peoples. Visit the archives of your worthiness. Bring food and stay awhile.

Bring your soul out to the plains of Sacredness. Kneel and praise earth and sky. Wash your spirit clean in holy water. Share breath with Creation. This pure air is deep ceremony. Drum your ancestors back to you. Sacredness will remind you, you are a sacred thing, too.

If you want to swim, it helps to be in the water. If you want freedom, spend your life in freedom spaces. Invest your soul in people whose soul water carries detectable levels of freedom. Each day, bathe in the sensation of your oneness with all things. This will keep you clean, pure, humble, and open to your noble work for the new day.

*Sun doesn't chase sunlight.
You shouldn't have to chase peace.*

Peace is in you. It is your very nature. When you chase peace out in the world, you abandon the peace you already are. Peace is not an acquisition. It is an excavation. Life's illusions have buried the peace in you. If your current condition is not peaceful, it doesn't mean you are not a peaceful person. Let go of that story. Release your false ideas about you and life, and you uncover your native peace. Go into that inner sunlight. Bask in yourself and all your peace.

Do not confuse your earthly condition with your true nature. You always were a beautiful thing. Maybe sky looks at you the way you look at sky. Consider yourself *that* big and beautiful. Rehabilitate your idea of yourself. This is the first brave movement into freedom. Once you see yourself as a phenomenal thing, you will permit yourself phenomenal things.

She erased all the social conditioning oppressing
her entire life and started over.

Deconditioning your mind from oppression is a long journey. You will need all your patience, all your ceremonies, all of your sacred Loving circle. Learning the *organic you* begins with unlearning all your invasive ideas of you.

When working to kill a virus, take all precautions to not become re-infected. Freedom work requires your wellness most of all. Your immune system must remain strong, resilient. Achieve this in your own wellness ways. Ceremony, ritual, community, family, nature, breathing, body work, remembering, resting, movement, inner stillness, releasing, purging, nurturing, Loving. Stay in your ways.

When you find yourself isolated among favored ones, with no one to relate to your reality, root yourself in thoughts of your Loved ones and all your relations. Dance, sing, drum if you can. Keep small ceremonies alive in that desolate space.

In the moments you feel peace, study the roots of its arrival. Repeat what brings you peace. Peace isn't random. It is a habit. It whispers something to us about the ways of being free. Strengthen your spirit's immune system to resist this supremacy contagion. What nourishes your soul? Do that. Do that for a lifetime.

Wellness is the greatest wealth we pass on to our children. The future ones are already alive in us, as a baby is in the womb, communicating in spirit ways how they feel about our choices, about our way of being. Already they are letting us know what kind of world they want us to leave for them. This is why in some moments we feel peace, in other moments we feel conflicted. When we know our way is wrong, it is because the future ones have let us know from their spirit womb in us that our way is wrong. We also feel their delight when our way is life.

Careful. Your way of being is not necessarily a way of life.
It may be a way of death.

Oppressive societies drown in their dreariness, in a social agreement to grimness. Freedom embraces the value of beauty, is not shamed by the decadence of simple pleasure even in the midst of suffering and struggle. Freedom does not say, *My cause is too serious for beauty.* Freedom says, *Because my cause is vital, let me savor beauty where I find its fortune. Let me taste every delicacy to suffuse my soul for this arduous labor of Love.*

Peace isn't to be bought, but soul-sought. It is an artifact of a soul well Loved. A remnant of healing, a pervasive flower risen from the ground of tenderness. If your oppressor lives in the center of your soul, it is time for a purging. A revolution overly waged out in the world will erode without daily inner contemplation, healing, and nurturing of the bonds within your revolutionary circle.

Does this set my soul free?
That is the question.

So many rivers in your life. Take the ones flowing to the ocean that is peace. Wash your spirit clean. Over and over. Choose freedom, a single quest that simplifies your life as all the cages come for you. Stay in your mantra question: *Does this set me free?* Be brave with the answer. And with your choices after. May you birth peace. And raise it beautifully. Here's to a glorious upbringing. And all your peaceful generations after. You are a worthy ancestor. Your offspring will flood this world forever.

Your pain is meant to be a compassionate catapult to a new reality, not a tar pit trapping you forever. Make sure your pain is working for you. It is your teacher. Your motive. Your movement. Your messenger. Make medicine with your sacred ache.

You may say, *First let me get well, then I will be ready to work for freedom.* Freedom says, *I will get you well. Work to get to me.*

Human perception is a cataract lens on the eye of this world. If you want to see clearly, expose your soul to the sunlight of truth. Risk eternal sunburn.

If you prefer giving your wealth to your oppressor, and not to your people, you have been overtaken by the slave virus. The inferiority virus. Consider whom you choose to feed. Cure your giving habits.

Feelings are your soul speaking to you. Don't run. Be a good listener. Make peace. Messages are coming through that want to heal you. Let them guide you to a beautiful life.

We do not have to surrender to the contagion of unkindness. In each moment we choose either freedom or the collective, conforming suffering of our times.

As you feed yourselves along your freedom road, it helps to learn the difference between nutritious freedom food and the slop offered by those who are out catching runaway slaves.

Your soul only wants soul food. Not junk food.
You have to cook if you want to burn.

If you want to be a candle of peace, open yourself to the high heat that is Truth. Be willing to be seasoned and baked by your journey, transformed by organic foods ripe with meaning. Make your mystic moments marinade for your manifest dreams. Feed your soul what it hungers for. Give it that and you will be free.

In some moments, freedom comes through union, immersion, or communion. In other moments, it arrives through solitude. Sometimes through both. Pay attention to what your soul craves. What you wanted in the womb is what you will want your whole life. Follow this river to the ocean of your sweet undoing.

In your quietest moments you are likely to be visited by clarity about your way forward in this work. Do not rush your silent visitor. Take the time. In this freedom endeavor, quietude, solitude, and stillness are sacred herbs, can be your special friend.

See beauty often. Everywhere. It keeps your revolution rooted in Love. It refreshes your soul water. Do not shy away from laughter. No sacred scroll has ever said your revolution must be grim.

It is possible to become consumed in being against or *anti* something, such that this something now controls our existence. We go where it goes, shift when it shifts, are dragged along by its impulses and whims, its tactics and strategies. We become soaked in its spirit, diluted of our essence, exhausted by its manipulations. We live in its shadow, neglecting our light. Its pathos overruns our inspiration, our vision making. Center your life in being *for* something. This way you control your daily directions, moods, and spirit. You are proactive, not reactive. Have faith in that which you are for. Pour into it. Believe it will do the work for you of acting against that which you are against. Grow an anchor, a compass, a self-determined root. Drink from your source. Stay in your sacred water. It has the power to manifest your freedom dream.

Have you gone wild yet today?
There's still time.
Put some freedom in your daily stew.

It is important that you repatriate your dreams. Your dreams get lost along the way. They lose their country. Which is your soul. Bring them back. Renew your hope and faith. Dare to believe your Love can make all things new.

Our struggle is not between belonging and loneliness. It is between abandonment and freedom. Do not abandon your own soul. Stay. You will know freedom.

REST FEEDS YOUR REVOULTION

Every single thing in your life
heals and blooms when you rest.

Your name is not exhaustion. You do not have to answer when called that way. Maybe exhaustion raised you at home. And exhaustion taught you at school. And exhaustion supervised you at work. And exhaustion was your Lover in relationships. Maybe you believe you are exhaustion. But, dear soul, you are not. You are life. A thing that breathes and releases and rests and sleeps and cries and crafts peace medallions from precious beads of moments. Even if all the people you have known have modeled exhaustion, you are not that species. You are a vibrant thing. Alive like spring meadows and freshwater sing. Blushing lotus, time to burn your false identity. You are not exhaustion. You are a winged thing shedding unnatural chrysalis, aloft toward bliss. You are diaphanous in sunlight. A bravery of spices. Pioneering stillness inside flocks of nervous geese. Powder blue flamingo adroit on silver water. Reunion with the code of Grace. You are not exhaustion. You reject that tragic race. No, priceless soul. You are not exhaustion. You are life. In Love with renewing your life. With a kiss. *Like this.*

Waging revolution takes immense energy from you. If you are not renewing yourself abundantly, continuously, you will exhaust yourself to death. If you are going to climb a mountain, bring food. If you cross a desert, bring water. If you jump into a volcano, insulate your body. And if you endeavor this freedom work, be passionate about your rest and restoration. However much you give yourself to servitude, give yourself at least that much to your wellness. Stay at the watering hole as long as you thirst. Stay in the shade until you are cooled. Remain in the intimate embrace of silence until your true voice returns. Nurturing your inner condition is a non-negotiable condition of revolution.

Don't be your own oppressor.
Rest. Rest. Rest.

Learn ease. Your life will go from exhausted productivity to vibrant fruitfulness. Exhausted, you drag negative spirit into the circle where your people live and breathe. Rested, you bring with you the sun itself. You bring sky. You bring life. Learn the power of *heartfulness* as a form of rest. If you grow weary as you serve others, do not blame them for your weariness. Open your heart to them even wider. Care deeply. *Compassion fatigue* is a popular term, yet it is a misnomer. Compassion does not fatigue. We do, when we abandon the infinite well of our compassion.

Would you rather get a hundred apples out of a tree for each of a few short years before it died of exhaustion, or forty apples a year out of the same tree for a hundred years? We aren't speaking of apple trees. We are speaking of you. Learn how trees stay free. Learn fruitfulness.

The most productive revolutionary activity of all is rest.

If the revolution tires you, such is the price for freedom. Slavery brings an exhaustion that makes revolution seem like a revival. If they can keep your body, mind, and spirit exhausted, they need no chains. Understand, your entire freedom depends on devoted rest. Make guilt-free rest your vocational calling. Do not segregate your rest. Let it flower all through your day.

If you are weary, rest.
If the thought of resting makes you anxious,
now you know why you are weary.

Please. No more working and doing yourself to death. Nothing about this is admirable. You know what is? Being healthy and available for your fullest life. We need you. Especially if you are contributing to a kind, compassionate, liberated, Loving world. New fad: renewal and balance. New role models: those who rest without shame or guilt. New culture: inner life. New you: peacefulness. Your new weather system: daily bliss.

Fatigue makes us want to surrender. This is why freedom workers need plentiful rest. Make rest the foundation of your revolution. More will get done. Not less. Sometimes, though, less needs to be done. Freedom breakthroughs can happen in the silence and respite in between roars.

We are so lost inside this unnatural way. When you grow tired, that is not a sign to push harder. It is a sign to let go of pushing. Remember peace, dear soul. Breathe deeply and remember peace. *Consuming-culture* creates a harsh, urgent desperation in the way we treat ourselves. Communal, earth culture births gentleness.

Sleep is a reboot for your brain. It clears all the file fragments, viruses, and damage accumulated during the day, protecting you from anxiety, depression, dementia, disease, and a broad host of human maladies. Don't treat sleep as a lazy inconvenience. That's cultural toxicity. Treat sleep like a lifesaving deep treatment for your frozen electronic device that holds every important file from your entire life. Supercharge your brain and being. Go to sleep.

Do you practice the excuse that you don't have time to rest? This is the classic, conditioned thought we use to neglect rest. If you lose your health, you will find more than enough time. Everything in our life is a matter of care and priority. We choose what to find time for. It doesn't take extraordinary time to close our eyes, exhale, and let our body release tension even for a few seconds. We spend cumulative hours on things that don't benefit us. A simple adjustment to our attitude about being well and valuing ourselves makes all the difference. You don't have to find the time. It's all around you.

Busyness is a cultural disease.
Cure yourself.

Simplicity blesses a revolution. To stay in touch with your growth journey and with your peace and clarity, practice asking yourself, *Does it nourish me?* The question, and the answer, can set you free. This is a way to develop spirit discernment, learning to see what is good for you and what is not. *Does it nourish me?* The question is a filter. It helps you purify your life. Here's to your soulful freedom. From all forms of oppression. Especially oppression of yourself. May you be nourished, you beautiful living thing.

Rest is a powerful and critical resource for a revolutionary. Profound rest requiring sacrifice of ways common in a supremacy society. Rest in the form of continuous shedding of social dynamics, rivers sourced from supremacy and flowing toward oppression. Continuous rejection and release of energy sapping oppression narratives. Rest that births true, restorative solitude and silence. Rest at the frequency of healing, whose womb is silence. Rest in virtually each moment of each day. It is not easy to learn to deeply rest in the midst of active living and human interaction. This takes devotion and commitment to restfulness. And to peacefulness, the cradle for rest.

Don't just pretend to rest. Rest is not a rehearsal. It is a sacred ceremony birthing your new life. Not physically working is not the same as resting, dear soul. If your mind still labors, your body still tires. Your nerves still fray. Your spirit still grows weary. Healthy societies honor renewal. Sick societies encourage exhaustion. Your guilt about resting enslaves your generations and makes your oppressor joyful. You need gatherings. Rest is a gathering for your soul. Make these things your lifestyle: *retreat, respite, solitude, quietude, contemplation, release, self-forgiveness, daydreaming*. *Re-womb* yourself. Let your mind fall into peace. You can learn to let go of the adrenaline-soaked tasking rope, and breathe. Practice letting go of the rope. Each time, reassure yourself: *I heal now so I can work more beautifully in the garden of my miraculous life.*

Exhaustion is not a requirement for being an admirable person. The only ones who benefit from your guilt about resting are those who have been exploiting your labor and body all along. When you break down, you and your Loved ones and circle of relations lose. When you wake up into your rightful restfulness, all your relations gain true wealth. Lost souls planted false seeds in your ancestors that have sprouted in you. Those seeds say one thing: *Do not rest.* Maybe, BeLoved, it is time to remove that generational story and plant new seeds. Maybe changing the world and birthing freedom begins with a deep breath, self-permission, and you resting into your natural, optimal, undepleted self. Maybe your best life is a rest life. Come taste this heavenly fruit.

She gave herself permission to rest.
Her soul said, Finally. *And gave her life.*

BeLoved, even a single, conscious breath is life-restoring rest. Sleep deprivation is killing us. Chronic adrenaline state is killing us. We believe we can work ourselves to life. Instead, we work ourselves to death. Value your life. Seek sacred balance. Remember, sleep is how the body and brain heal, purge, and prevent disease. Rest is the foundation for fruitfulness. If you want life, behave like all other living things, and rest. You will have life.

People will come, ravenous for the fruits of your labor. Then grow to feel entitled to your labor. You are not a plow. You are not a plow horse, meant to strain until you die. You are abundance and its way into this world. Protect your vessel. You are an entire field of beauty, meant for an abundant life.

You do not rest only for you. You rest for everyone, everything. Resting is not selfish. It is communal. You rest for your ancestors, because they couldn't. You rest for your descendants, so you may leave them a more nourishing world. You rest for all living things, so you may be medicine and not a destroyer. You rest for the birthing of dreams. You rest to remember. You rest to bring us back to sacredness. When you rest, your restfulness exudes out into the community, into the circle. We take on your restful energy and give it back to you, deepened by our collective restfulness. When you rest, you are contributing your wealth into the collective wealth. You are making a social offering. Please, you priceless treasure. Bless us with rest.

We used to rest together. Naturally and in rhythm with each other. Without protocols or programs, we would listen to our great teachers, our bodies, and instinctively lie down together in our homes, in courtyards, under trees, in meadows, by cool streams and rustling willows, wherever we were. This ceremony was a root for our togetherness. It kept us well. No one was self-conscious about resting because everyone rested. And because we rested, everything else in our lives was richer, more robust and fertile. Rest calmed us through life's ups and downs. We were not depressed or anxious, because our hormonal river was regulated. We were more patient, kind, creative. More present, attentive, aware, sensitive. More fruitful in our labor. We were more alive. It is important for us to understand, this restful way of being was violently taken from us by souls who wanted to exploit our wellness, to turn it into a soulless, indentured labor for their material gain. The reason we no longer rest together is because our togetherness was too beautiful for those hungry ghosts to bear. They had to destroy it. Yet we remain. We need to remember now that we used to rest together. It is our heritage. Can you remember this? If you can grow still and quiet, the memories may wake in you: those days when we were peaceful and lay down together on earth's maternal chest. To rest. As though it were the most natural, life-giving thing. Because it was.

Productivity is a way of life obsessed with *product*, even to the detriment of life. It begs for burnout. Its natural endpoint is depletion of resources, actual extinction of the material world. Productivity conditions us into a phobic relationship with the world. Everything is a potential threat to our urgent, possessive quest to produce. We become desecrators of everything sacred, because Sacredness cannot be exploited until we make it not sacred. This is how we desecrate even ourselves. For ultimately we view our own being, our bodies and other aspects as highly accessible resources for our insatiable hunger. We cannibalize ourselves to be productive. Fruitfulness, in contrast, is a way of life devoted to fruit, always to the benefit of life. Fruit as natural yield from natural cycles of sustenance living. In fruitfulness we value all the fruits of life. We see all fruits as existing in close relation, a seeing that helps us keep our life elements in relative balance and harmony. Fruitfulness endears soul into union with the world. We become nurturers and birthers, protectors and healers of living things. Our relationship to resources mirrors our relationship with ourselves: *philic*, not phobic. We experience the world not as a threat or exploitable commodity, but as a thing we Love, cherish, and therefore honor. May your revolution be fruitful.

A culture that encourages you to do more, to the point of exhaustion and illness, is not evolved. Practice doing less without guilt and watch how your life grows fertile and free. The more you are marginalized by society, the more society guilts you into doing more. You become fearful of being labeled lazy, unproductive, valueless, inferior, unworthy, undesirable, undeserving. To free yourself of this conditioned slavery, to ignite self-Love in your soul, try this mantra: *I have the human right to do less. Doing less, I am enriched with health, rest, peace, balance, and fruitfulness. I am enough. I do enough. I achieve enough. My life, my being, my existence are enough.*

I am deeply empathic.
Therefore I rest.

If you are deeply empathic, you get this. You are doing soul labor in every moment that others aren't. You cannot afford to measure your rest against theirs. Even for them, many are exhausted and dying. For you, feel, rest, stay alive. Grant yourself permission for quiet, calm, stillness, peace in bushels. No guilt or shame to your resting game. They will slave you to death. Break that generational oppression chain. Your candle burns intensely. You need more wick. Your life force is that wick. Renew it continuously. Your deep feeling, intuitive nature requires that you become a sayer of No. No to giving more, doing more, dying more. Beautiful, Loving, honoring, respectful No's. Flocks of No's that give birth to Yes's. Yes to retreat, renewal, restoration, refill, recharge, rebirth. Romance your rest. Learn to rest through it all. Rest when you are alone. Rest immersed in a sea of souls. Rest in spirit even when you are with community, family, friends, and your wilderness ancestors. Look up at the sky, exhale and rest. Imitate a tree and rest. Rest is your treasure chest. Each time you open it, jewels of blessing. Not stressing or pressing. Resting. Rest as you listen, guide, nurture, lead, and comfort. Rest while you sleep. You think you're smooth, pretending sleep, deep feeling your way through the night. Let it go. Drop down into the peace sleep beyond concern and let your entire being heal. You are a healer, a feeler, a deep dealer. So say it until you live it: *I confess, I am at my best and blessed when I rest.*

Some species are so exhausted from gestating, birthing, caring, or building, they die after their offering. You are not one of them. Rest, birth, rest, care, rest, build, rest again, dear one. Rest joyfully. Jubilantly. As though you have every right. Because you do. A sustainable life is one in which you rest abundantly. You are making a whole new world, restoring the ancestral ways. Not by doing. By resting all the way back to your full power. Let your faithful brain heal. Let your dutiful body heal. Let your loyal heart heal. Let your brazen spirit heal. Let your whole life heal. Make that your offering. Show us the freedom way.

If you want to help heal the world, slow down. Breathe, you precious treasure. In your frenetic daily rushing, you outrun even your own spirit. You need your spirit to stay in Spirit, your place and source of discernment and true seeing. Lose this and you become harmful to yourself and the world. Those who want to profit from the world's chaos, from humanity's confusion, need you to keep rushing. That way, you won't be seeing. Or being. Only doing. Addicted, chronic doing is a critical epidemic. You can feel it in the air around you. Everywhere humans are or have been. It is contagious. Keep your soul's immune system strong. Stay in your spirit: Stillness. Silence. Rest. Contemplation. Breathing. Loving. Stay in your spirit. This is how you make medicine with your holy life.

HELP YOUR PEOPLE HEAL

In the beginning you may fight your way to freedom. In the end, you heal your way to freedom. The outer condition of oppression becomes an inner condition in a flash. The inner condition is the final shackle to remove. If not, apparent social freedom collapses back in on itself, returning to slavery like a chick to its nest.

Healing is not always polite.
It speaks the Truth.

Name the supremacies that ail us. Be specific. The more vague our language, the more we invite the sickness to harbor itself, latent and spawning, in our linguistic hiding places. Call out the pathology. It will slither into its hideouts. But it will have been touched by the eviction notice of social attention.

Living under the chronic stress and hostility of oppression can, especially over generations, create an intense way of being. A perpetual crisis condition that wears down health, vitality, relations, dreams, and creative fruitfulness. Freedom work and revolutions are creative acts. They depend on joy and warmth along the way. When a people grow tense, intense, and cold, to themselves and each other, this steals vital elements from the liberation journey. It is challenging to live in a relaxed, fluid condition when your social conditions assault you. Freedom's path is to convince yourself of your intrinsic wellness while still in the clutches of a social spirit that is not well.

Brokenness that does not discover purpose in its brokenness remains broken. If it fails to believe in that purpose, it teeters endlessly between promise and brokenness. It summons the will to act on that promise, or it remains a slave to brokenness.

Gardeners and farmers know they don't do the growing. The plants do that. Don't be afraid to call yourself a healer. You know you don't do the healing. Souls do that.

Fear, guilt, and shame are shackles used to enslave you. With your people, discover what elements dissolve those shackles. Then pour with all your might. To appreciate freedom, let yourselves feel the pain, the acid truth of your enslavement.

Go to destitute places where there seems to be no soul and bleed out your soul. Let it gush and weep and stain every surface. Where there is little spirit, rain down your spirit. Monsoon without apology. Where Love is lacking, be obscene in the nudity of your sunlight. Do not despair what is missing in the world. Cherish your chance to give it.

Oppressed condition is a scar tissue. Freedom is the breaking of that tissue over and again. Scar tissue always wants to grow back. Persist applying freedom.

If you spend too much of your life trying to convince society that you and your kind are fully human, you can lose touch with your human life. You can become an announcement undrenched in its own soul waters. An advertisement, a broadcast. A roaming ghost. Spend your life being. Let the light and language of *that* speak for you and yours. Emanate your sacredness. Role model your revolution.

Every living thing that goes unexercised withers, weakens, and dies. Every human requires the exercising of their humanity. Otherwise we grow cold, hollow, dispassionate. We become ghosts simply going through the motions. Use your humanity or lose your humanity. Practice being a strand in the web of living things.

Freedom spirit in human groups does not say, *When we get free it's going to be so good.* It says, *When we get good, it's going to be so free.* Healing is the centerpiece to undo the undoing of free souls. To stir the spirit wick back to light and life.

No matter what you go through, you have power. When you breathe deeply, you are strong. When you cry, you are strong. When you reach out for help, you are strong. When you express your heart creatively, you are strong. Let your pain raise you. Not like a child. Like a mountain.

See if the flame of your soul candle leans toward freedom.
If it does not, open a soul window. Change the draft.

Status quo is a massive dead sun exerting its immeasurable gravity on all bodies. Holding them in a soulless destitution and allegiance. To pull free from this force, let us grow deliriously in Love with our freedom dream. As we become sufficiently feverish, reason falls away. Without reason, we are ready to be baked. Transformed. To endure the changes in our practical lives and mystic imagination necessary to be inside the great freedom burn.

The way past the pain is through the pain.
That's where the medicine is. Taste the fruit.

Generational pain is not punishment. It is an opening. You are a people rich in doors. Step through them. Rich in windows. Look through them. Rich in wombs and births. Drink your raw wonder of being so new. Nurse on the milk of your millennia. Your age is here.

Who can know how much tenderness from how many ancestors we carry? Hesitation is our tenderness saying, *All this is new.* Because it is new. In each moment you are a baby learning to walk. Embrace the wobble, breathe peace. Soon you will be the sturdiness of old trees and ancestor-mountains who know their majesty.

Affirm yourself until you believe the affirmation. Then affirm your belief until it becomes a living affirmation. Your thoughts and beliefs are not random. They are the children of repetition. Repeat yourself all the way to the beautiful life your soul envisioned before this world. Affirm until you believe. Believe and you shall be affirmed.

If you have been violated for centuries, or a lifetime, holding boundaries around your sacredness can feel terrifying. As though by prohibiting violation, you are losing your tether to life. Introduce yourself to your own sovereignty the way you would introduce your child to safe touching. Teach yourself the lesson gently, repeatedly. Say the holy words.

Know that the wrath of slaves and slave owners will come for you as you do this work, as you indulge this Love affair. Fortify yourself daily with your kin. Nurture and strengthen each other.

Like a cow grazing only the idea of grass, many of us much prefer an imitation of freedom to the actual thing itself. We want the candy but not the cotton. We want the fruit of labor, but will destroy all fruit if it means we do not have to labor. The only thing that gets a squatting, protesting animal to move is the sight and scent of whatever it is starving for. If you want your people to get up and move, feed them the end of pain. Dangle it before them from the stick of freedom.

Conflict between oppressed peoples comes from a displacement of wounds and wound energy. Each person latching on to whatever crumb they feel is an aspect of power, when it is not power at all, just more invasive oppressor conditioning.

An impactful, enduring revolution needs to overcome the human tendency toward tribal delineation and conflict. The

Us versus *Them* virus is nearly as destructive as the supremacy virus.

Once people realize that ending their lifestyle of pain is the only way to end their life of pain, some will change their lifestyle and receive new life. Others will clench their lifestyle tighter and blame your revolution for their life of pain. Your work is to nurture your lifestyle so that whoever looks upon it catches a new light in the soul, and is inspired to transform the style of their life.

Reparation efforts by oppressors and their favored kind are often based not on understanding but on guilt. When the fumes of guilt dissipate, a residue remains. Its name is resentment. Only self-reckoning creates a feeling of true personal culpability. This feeling inhibits resentment of the truth that something is owed. That something is to be offered, from within the self, first and most of all. People act to repair harm in the world when they are clear their life duty is to do so, regardless of who did what to whom. A society can never offer oppressed people enough material benefits to justify its oppression of their kind. Comfort is not an antidote for enslavement. Reparation comes through the soulful transformation of society in a direction away from its soul sickness. Wealth and wellness follow the course of that river.

In an oppressive society, everyone's foot is on the neck of unfavored people. Even the foot of other unfavored people. If you are a people who have come through genocide, it is not enough to regain your footing. Will yourselves to remove the foot from your neck that has held you to the mud and mire. Otherwise you go on living in a bent-over state, contorted and afraid to stand tall closer to the sun. Once you have regained footing, you can take flight. This is how the ancestral drumbeat calls us to the fire for healing.

So that what has been ground to dust may divinely rise again.

Genocide spreads lies as to a people's right to exist in their own manner. Lies that invade souls like viruses. Eradicate this virus that says your people have no right to live. Counter genocide with a wild, passionate existence dance.

If we wish to be free, we reclaim our own languages. Language affirms the soul with every word. It is medicine. We reclaim our own ways. Our ways were what made us in the first place. Ritual, ceremony, practice, values, rhythms, and stories hold us in a self-Loving embrace. We garden our own stories. Harvest our own food.

To let the discomfort and displeasure of your oppressor dictate your self-expression, determination, change efforts, or existence is to agree to remain chained and subdued. Do not be complicit in your own enslavement. Leave the enabling and pleasing of your abuser behind. Care more about your people living a beautiful life.

Freedom revolutions are, in the beginning and end, an inward work. A private reckoning. Because such revolts have social cause and roots, they sweep us continuously into outward currents. Into *they-ing* and *them-ing* and *we-ing* and *us-ing*. We need time in these dimensions. Though to remain there, we lose hold on the inward vine, the soul current that keeps us clear and intact. In your leadership role, your opportunity is to facilitate maintenance of the balance between inward and outward focus, healing, and growth. Direct the symphony along its delicate course.

The social core still festers to this day. If you squeeze it hard enough, the festering comes through. In some eras, the festering runs through from core to skin, like the rotted fruit from a strange harvest. No squeeze is needed to see the ugliness. You can see it plain and from a distance. In other times, many wish to believe we are healed through and through. But the core still festers. Ugliness is still capable of raising up and killing any threat to its nesting place—a society un-reckoned, a heritage not truly or fully admitted, an inner heart unexposed. The festering breeds in a cocoon of denial, avoidance, rationalization, minimization, of selective forgetting. Caste systems don't stand erect like buildings. They are organic sludge repeatedly repaired by active illness and passive submission to those who maintain the ignoble structures.

The young man had been taught to suffocate his feelings, which caused him pain. Slowly, he took the brave journey of learning to become a fountain. It caused him peace.

Healthful emotional release is a life skill that carries us from struggle and self-harm to ease and wellness. All that flows through us must flow from us. We can learn to do this beautifully, so we may water the world and all our relations. Human social revolutions are mighty rivers that begin with the release of private obstructions. May you not resist your precious flowing nature. Release your many waters in a good way. Make an abundant ceremony of your life.

You will not be able to scold people into freedom. Between healthy, caring adults, scolding is not necessary. It is an artifact we picked up in childhood. And when you were scolded as a child, how did your tender heart feel? *Exactly.* This is how we raise people who do not Love themselves. Who feel they are a failure no matter what. It is also how we raise people who only know how to relate and communicate

113

in a hurtful, shaming way. Together, let us choose to leave behind the culture of power and control, and claim a nurturing way. Our words, tone, body language, and expressions are so very powerful and long impacting. Let us use this power as medicine for every soul.

Maybe nurturing ourselves in relation to all living things is a deeper kind of self-care, a mutual care that infuses us with the Love energy and life spirit flowing through the world. Maybe self-care that deeply touches our social purpose is the medicine we need. Possibly, we are here to make of our lives an offering to the collective, the way trees through their roots offer their nutrients to the forest. Maybe our focus on self can be a form of our soul's focus on the collective. A way of inviting humanity to gather with us. Maybe we genuinely need each other. If we could find ways to find each other sacredly, maybe our self-Love would grow real roots. It would not be fleeting or conditional. It would be rich and enduring as earth. It is ironic that in our individualistic cultures we are so lonely and seek to cure this loneliness through a focus on the self. Maybe self-focus is our timid first step in acknowledging our communal needs. Maybe we are relearning to extend a meaningful invitation to community. One that says, *Welcome into my life. I feel like we need each other. Together, let us grow beyond domination and control. Let us rediscover ancestral togetherness. Let us weave the sacred blanket of belonging again. You can be safe with me. I hope I can be safe with you. Welcome, into my life.*

She wove her self-Loving thoughts into a blanket.
Then she taught her sisters how to weave.

May we teach each other how to weave healing and wellness. Let us reclaim our true, intrinsic medicine, an act of liberation and freedom. Weave your sacred blanket. Wear it out. Keep reweaving. Gather in healing circles. Break the bread of soul story. Eat plenty. Stay warm by the fire of communion, kindness, remembering. Endure until the hope of dawn. Ride that rising light.

GATHER YOUR PEOPLE

You aren't just a person. You are a people.
Gather your nation. Gather your power.

Oppressive cultures discourage community gatherings and spaces. They know gathering is blood-soul flow and breath. Without it, the organ that is a people dies. Resist your oppressor's discouragement for your gathering. Be more determined to gather when you face resistance. Resistance is a sign that your gathering has medicine, potential, and promise for your people.

Gathering is how you create safe spaces for your people. Gather in the spaces and moments conventional, oppressive life offers. But make sure to gather in all the ways wild things do. Gather at midnight by singing brooks casting moonlight. Gather in the territory of wolves. Gather for long hours, eating slowly, talking story to candlelight or fire. Gather in response to tragedy, as an offering to grief. Gather in person, or in spirit at a distance. Reject authoritative, soulless, task-obsessed gathering. This is not gathering. It is mass dying. Gather as Lovers. Bring all your tears. Bring your grass baskets filled with ancestral seeds of testimony. We need new gardens. Bring the sacred smoke of your hope and prayers. Bring your entire harvest of wisdom and pain. Bring the fruit of your true soul labor. Invite the doulas, birthers of life and vitality. Bring the elders, bring them to the center of the circle. Arrange for the children to sit near their grandparents. We are gathering for our generations to touch each other. They need the scent of seasons. Gather in trees, on mountains, deep in the heart of valleys. Gather in twos, dozens, hundreds, thousands, millions. Gather in silence and in song. Gather like lightning bugs. Blister night sky in brilliance. Gather like water after rain. Drop by drop move over earth and barrier until you find each other and become puddle, pond, lake, river, ocean. Gather the way you gathered as children in summer. So alive with the moment and swept together by Love and adventure that all else not of your gathering glory is swept away. They will not want you to gather. They will scheme and plot for ways to prevent or end your gathering. They will send spies and scouts and scour the perimeter, squinting into your gathering through looking glasses cataract-hazed with the film of supremacy's sickness. The hungry ghosts will peer through their clouded lenses but they will not see you. For you will have transformed together into pure soul. And you will be a sacred thing, untouchable and on fire with diaphanous flame.

As soon as your space is deemed of value to your people, your oppressors will deem it of value for them to acquire. To rename, remake, and sell as though they alone had created it. If they cannot have it, they will destroy it. Fear can only overtake you when you have abandoned Spirit, the source of your sacred space. If they keep their spaces impotent of Spirit, it is because Spirit is the wildest thing of all. It will never be controlled. They don't want that. Can't afford that. If, in your worship spaces, your very spirit feels oppressed, maybe that is not your natural worship space. Maybe it has become their place of crowd control.

When you are kind to a stranger, that touch is a form of gathering. Acknowledging each other is a gathering. Sharing Loving energy is a gathering. Do not follow your oppressor's rigid ways of scheduling gathering. They will keep your gatherings scarce. Gather like wild things. Spill gatherings out into your life as a flood of purification and remembering. When we gather together in a Loving way, even our worst hurt can seem just a little smaller.

Notice how your oppressor grows nervous when you are singing, dancing, relaxed, and joyful. Especially if your people are gathered in this condition. This condition is freedom. Your oppressor needs you in chains and cages of tension, heaviness, stress, anxiety, fear. These chains draw you into yourself in a defeated isolation from your people. Or into a shared surrender with your people. But when you grow joyful and expressive, you summon your ancestors and threaten the plantation-reservation arrangement. You overcome false supremacy, for *you joyful is you in Love.* Your Love is supreme.

Go naked into the smoke lodge under moonlight and weep. Weep in song and story. Tell the story of your journey. What meaning you have gathered. Your grief and hope. Your Love and learnings. Pass the talking stick. Circle around your children and elders. Leave room for your ancestors. Open to Grace and Spirit. Stay in that warm womb long and deep. Be willing to be born. As many times as it takes for freedom.

Don't arrive at gatherings like a dead thing, on automatic. Arrive like fire. Be all the way present, alive, ready to burn away what needs to be shed, to prepare the ground for new seed. Arrive in full-throated song. Arrive dancing and drumming. Arrive as all your people. You aren't at the gathering for you. You are there for all of us. Ancestors should swirl around you. Ceremony ought to drip from your skin. Water teachings flooding from your eyes. All your Love should be at high tide. You should be a tidal wave. Or a gentle sand soaking up Truth. Or a coral reef protecting your people and all living things. When you join a gathering, pry yourself open and pour out medicine. Your whole life has been the pestle and mortar grinding moments to paste and powder. Don't be stingy. Make your offering.

Learn the freedom programs.
Burn the freedom programs.
Learn your soul.

Build together. Freedom schools and programs. Freedom content and archives. Freedom stories. Freedom gatherings and initiatives. Freedom ceremonies and rites of passage. Freedom relationships. In all of this, graduate past indoctrination. Make the programming compostable. Nurture people into their own form of freedom.

It is a rare soul who crawls up out of the grave of slavery into the sunlight of freedom and stays there. If you are on this quest, make sure to gather your many suns. Stay close.

We can relearn how to pour our various forms of wealth into our circle of relations who Love and care for us. Who we Love and care for. This is a vital habit of free souls, an essential course for freedom.

If your people gather, drum, sing, dance, cry, remember, pray, talk story, hear your ancestors, learn from your elders, let the children speak, share food and wealth in the old way, and stay in your ceremonies, you can be free.

If hungry ghosts with ropes and chains and treaties and funding arrive, smiling and saying they are your friends, gather all you hold dear and all your people and build a freedom fire.

Those who are threatened when two or more of you gather are dependent on your absence from the spaces they inhabit, your absence from all spaces, in order to feel life is in order. Destroy this order. Gather. Gather not in spite, but in Love for yourselves.

Rather than seek to purify the air your oppressor has polluted, fill yourselves with a new air, from a fresh, unpolluted source. If this requires new spaces, migrate to them or create them. Be willing to start from blessed scratch.

Oppression enjoys weaponizing shame. Shame is a bully. Weak once you stand your ground. Back it down simply by being true to you. Gather your people. Be you together.

No more meetings, trainings. Only gatherings. No more conferences, presentations, agendas, and zombies in seats. Only passion gathered around a fire, drumming, dancing, singing, each soul pitching its branches into the flames. Only freedom.

When you do gather, they will try to control the way you gather. They will say, *Sit this way. Gather this way. Don't move too much, don't feel too much, don't speak the truth, don't use uncomfortable words. Don't show your power. Don't socialize too long, too deep, too secretly. Don't leave us out. Don't single us out. Don't do the don'ts we've taught you. Don't drum, sing, dance, remember, rise.* And you will ask why, and they will say, *Because our way is supreme, of course. And we've all been doing it this way for years.* Truth is, they are terrified of anything that wakes the soul.

Bodies are easily enslaved. So too the mind. Spirit can be a willful horse. But they break it by breaking your relations.

This is why you gather. In safe spaces, not polluted with fear. This is why you increase your singing, dancing, drumming, praying, passage rites, ceremony.

Among earth cultures, celebration is not about superficial festivity. To celebrate means to dance to the truth, sing to the truth, speak to the truth. It is a reunion with the core of life. A reminder of who we are and not who others say we are. It is a confirmation. A validation. A re-commitment. A giving of thanks. Honoring. Remembering. Cleansing. Preparation for the next steps down the path. Earth cultures celebrate often. Not superficially. Wisely. And from the soul.

When the world falls apart, you are blessed with a new window through which to see what truly matters: *a way for the world to rise together.* When the surreal becomes true life and the old illusions fall, take your opportunity to see what is real. Make that your life. Now is the time to gather your relations in spirit and Love. Light a fire. Talk story. Render beauty. Sacred blanket each other in goodness. Paint the night in a hopeful poetry. And when morning comes, no matter how difficult, soulrise into the world. Be a ceremony of compassion, a fountaining ambassador of Grace.

YOUR ANCESTORS AND YOU

When you feel less than beautiful, remember. You are the beadwork adorning your ancestors. Your soul is their sacred jewelry. The way turquoise and silver catch sunlight is the way your radiance beautifies their life inside you. Many hands placed your beads. You are more than decoration. You are the freedom story your old ones are telling the world.

It is possible your ancestors were in their lifetimes some blend of oppressor and oppressed. Rather than run from this contradiction that sparks shame in you, embrace it. Inside your heritage and soul are both the teacher and student of freedom. Let the perpetrator in you teach and learn from its own ways. And the part of your being that is bruised by oppression, let that part of you teach and take the masterclass.

Your ancestors outnumber your fears.
Feel your power.

You are greater than you will ever know. All the people of all your people are lifting you up in spirit and Love. Your fear is a dying ash compared to that eternal fire. You are not alone. This is the lie they tell you to keep you weak and down. You are the mountain, each ancestor its grain of earth. Stand at the peak, near sun and sky, and release your power. A power to heal our world. A power to let your gift rumble out, a free herd of bison reclaiming the land. You don't seek our sacred ways. You hold them in your riverbed of memory. Set them free. Release our teachings back to the people. Feel your power. Live in it. Make medicine with your holy life.

How to gather your ancestors: Make offerings. Pour water. Start with your tears. Burn the plants. Kneel to the earth. Grow silent and still. Find your true heart. Open it. Remember your true soul. Remember peace. Speak to them. They will speak to you. *Listen.* When you see wind moving the trees, those are your ancestors dancing on the leaves. Cry joy. If you want to hear your ancestors clearly, prepare a space for them: *inner quiet.*

They will say, *Don't blame me for what my ancestors did*. This places the act in the past, absolving them of guilt and accountability. The crime was not just committed. It is still being done. It is a present doing. To spew out, *I have nothing to do with what my ancestors did to yours*, is a self-serving and destructive mentality. In fact, it is not even self-serving. It is self-defeating. To conceive that the suffering of others is not a part of your own suffering is the kind of fragmented-world perception that ails favored and unfavored people both. Each of us is the continuation of not only our ancestors, but also of the lives that they lived. Their lives created ripples in the fabric of generations. Ripples that become the very cultural ground we walk on and air we breathe, from the very first moments of our conception. Their attitudes are passed down to each succeeding generation. In the case of prejudice and dehumanizing ideas, this is a waterfall foul and stench.

Say to those who reject any responsibility for their ancestors: Your body is the body of your ancestors. Your spirit is a hand-me-down weaving from your ancestor's spirit cloth. The way you think, move, think, feel, see, react, speak, behave, exist, all derive from your ancestor crops. Your familial ancestors and your social, cultural ones. You are not determined by your ancestors, though truly you reflect them. Your blood, tears, temperament, and orientation toward the world, all of this in part you inherited from those who came before. You cannot disclaim yourself from your ancestors' legacy or energy. You can only honor the good they left, heal the harm they left. You are not an individual suddenly appearing in the world without generational influence. You cannot take that escape route. When we speak of your ancestors, we are not speaking of the past. We are speaking of them alive now in you. Consciously or not, you carry out their way of life. You *are* your ancestors. Make peace with that. So this world can be at peace with you.

Our Eternals, the ancient ones, left simple instructions:
Come to this earth and make an offering of your life.

Your ancestors are not an imaginary thing. You are an imaginary thing until you reunion with your ancestors. Your ancestors make you a soulful thing in this tangible world. Your ancestors will kill your fear. You do not have to call your ancestors to you. They are in you. Always with you. Always trying to get out to speak out. To live freely through you as they were not able to do in their earth time. If you kneel by the water and look deeply into it with your spirit eyes, you will see your ancestors. When it feels they are not with you, it is only because you are not with you. Be with yourself. This is a freedom practice that brings you deep companionship and peace.

Your ancestors live now, in nature. If you don't know how to access your ancestors it may be because you have lost your nature. Go touch something living. Do this until you feel comfortable with living things. Sky, breeze, water, earth, sun, stone, plant, animal, insect, microbe, yourself. When was the last time you were present enough to deeply feel the energy and sensation of your own body? Your body is your sovereign territory. Walk the land.

Healing ancestral wounds requires spending plentiful time with your ancestors. How do you support the healing of a child's trauma? You spend abundant time together doing a lot of listening, talking, reassuring, hugging, crying, playing, creative expressing, laughing, remembering, reflecting, praying, ceremony, and whatever else are the child's healing ways. Your ancestors, alive in you, require the same time and nurturing. Soulless, oppressive, individualistic culture may have conditioned you to believe ancestors are not a real thing, just a superstition from *uncivilized* cultures. This then is the first wound for you to heal. For if you do not believe your ancestors are alive in you, you surely cannot heal ancestral wounds. Healing together in community is powerful medicine. Gather and talk story with your kindred kind. Touch the wounds your ancestors were oppressed into not touching. Speak and name the wounds they were unable to give language to. If you hold these old wounds in your hands and reassure them of your Loving presence, attention, and care, like a distressed baby or child in your cradling arms, those wounds begin to feel comforted. Those wounds begin to calm, drift to sleep, regenerate into wholeness energy, and heal. Gather. Touch. Cradle. Sing. Drum. Dance. Talk story. See forward into your vision of what life can be. Your ancestors have so much to say about their journey and yours. They will squabble as usual. Listen to their squabbling. And when the sun of a new day rises above the horizon of your long shared pain, take your ancestors' hands in yours and walk together into that verdant valley of freedom. Your shared tears will create rivers of gratitude. Love's offering will be water. Follow the flow home. Let your eternal ones join you in your Promised Land. After all, they first dreamed it for you.

It is up to you to call the pure soul of your ancestors to you, to flavor your spirit for the task. Their imperfection in life, hold that in your heart for a true reckoning, then let it pass. But even in life they possessed a purity in the soul, an astounding sap at their soul center. Call that to you. Let it flush out your innerness. If you go walking in the woods you pick up pollen on your skin. Walk through the wilderness of your ancestors. Pick up the dander of their divinity. Let that be your protection and power for what you have to do now as you become an ancestor. Praise their holy names.

Do we really feel that everything *positive* that we have in our lives is the exclusive consequence of our own individual character and striving? That our social status, and the material and social wealth of our family and community, have nothing to do with wealth and status of the generations before us and how they acquired that status and wealth? We are grand inheritors. Whether what we inherit is human-affirming or human-destroying is not so important as our realization and reckoning with the degree to which we inherit. This recognition is the moment that opens the doorway toward personal and collective healing.

The uninspired tribal chant, *I have nothing to do with what happened to your ancestors. Don't blame me for what my ancestors did*, renders people incapable of treating the ongoing oppression wound. Wounds untreated do not remain the same. They fester. This kind of festering leaches health, vitality, fruitfulness, soulfulness, and humanity from the world.

Historical oppression is not an extinct species because it is historical. It remains alive and with us *because* it is historical. Its old roots make for a strong, living supremacy tree. Strange fruit grows there not only because of what happened in the past, but largely because today's social climate remains optimal for the tree. If you want to kill a thing, alter the climate for which it is suited. Your revolution frames itself in the past. Its work is within the weather of today.

My soul a soil carrying the seeds of my ancestors.
So many forests yet to rise up from me.

Nurture relationship with the collective goodness of your ancestors. The descendants of oppressors may feel shame about their ancestors. This is a sign they have not met with their ancestors and reckoned. Until they take personal responsibility for cleansing themselves of their ancestors' oppressive inheritance, they cannot be free of deeper suffering. And if you are a descendant of oppressed ancestors, make peace with their wounded ways. Forgive their trespass against their own sacredness. Claim that your ancestors originated in goodness, in health and beauty. Say this is who you come from, who you are. Claim the soulful essence of your heritage. Make it known within you so it is the aura by which you introduce yourself.

Cursed be the children of slaves. Cursed be the children of slaveholders. Cursed be the children of all those who stood by the fence and beheld the horror of humankind. None shall be untouched by this darkness. None shall walk free of this most wicked imprint upon the ground and spirit of earth. There will surely be those in days beyond the original season, those who express no claim to these *undoings* of the soul. Cursed be them most of all. This virus is a living dust on every windowsill. To end this curse, a soul must cry remorse and let the tears of reckoning be a medicine of the heart.

Until the kindred descendants of slave masters kill the spirit sickness of their ancestors still vibrant in them, until they eradicate supremacy and oppression in their ways and culture, they will suffer a soulful, spiritual, psychic pain greater even than the kindred descendants of slaves.

A person's holistic health is a radiation from the seeds of self-idea. Healthy self-idea cannot be achieved without integrity between a person's past and present in a generational sense, which then allows for the fulfillment of a person's future. Know your ancestors and your descendants in any way you can.

Take great care how you treat the world. You are becoming an ancestor even as you take this next breath. Ancestry is not in your age or expiration date. It is in the purification or polluting of your heart and spirit. These are the legacies and legends you leave this world.

What would your life look like if you lived in a culture where rest and wellness were your foundation, relationships mattered more than greed and liability, and work was your rhythmic, organically timed vocation? A life where resources were sustainable, poverty did not exist, your health didn't depend on wealth, all people had dignity and noble purpose, and children were safe from adults? Such societies do exist. *Advanced* societies call these ways and people primitive. You may call them your ancestral ways. *Remember.*

The eternals, your ancestors, are with you in a Loving way. They are not neutral. Whatever their imperfections in life, they have changed to light. They see the light. In all things. In you. They want you well and free. You can trust their whispers to your soul.

Envision your ancestors praying for a better day. Now recognize. *You are* their better day. Regard your life more highly. Rejoice. Hope is a short term key to long-term healing. Choose to be hopeful. Practice hopefulness. If you grow still enough inside your hope, you can hear your ancient ones cheering you on. They have seen the full journey of life and have forgiven themselves. This is why they see you and see the glory your guilt and shame keep you from seeing. You see? You are already worthy of being celebrated. You are now in your lifetime, which is a sacred thing. Wake each morning and say, *Somebody once dreamed of all the beauty I get to live today. Troubles or not, my life is that better day.*

CARE FOR YOUR SACRED STORIES

Take care of your sacred stories.
They are the garden of your life.

Hope is the light bursting out from the story you tell yourself. Despair is when your story chases all the light away. Mend your story. Stories too can tire and fray. Hope habits are what make hopeful people hopeful. These habits require practice. We have to build our hope muscles for times of heavy lifting. The more oppressed and dehumanized you and yours are, the more hopeful you must become. This is the sacred dance. Weave a hopeful story. Carry your whole life in that basket. Hard times are like a cold night just before a brilliant dawn. *Storytell* your personal sunrise.

She who stops telling herself nightmares and starts
telling herself fantasies, shall live in paradise.

Whose story are you telling yourself all day long? Likely one you inherited. Burn your old stories whose voice sounds like trauma. The gloom and doom. The fear and doubt. Start a fresh new you tale that spa-treats your soul. Your life is not about your circumstances. It is about the legend you create in your mind that invades your soul, soaks your heart, and floods out into your life. Harness the power of your storytelling to make your sweet dreams come true. No more nightmares. Only fantasies. You're in paradise now, dear one. Time for a paradise kind of mentality.

Speak your truth. Say what you truly mean. Coded language serves those who destroy. Naked language serves our ultimate healing. In an oppressive society, code language is developed that protects favored people from guilt, shame, and culpability. Break through this insulation by speaking precise truth. Call the diseases by their true names. Name the perpetrators. Describe not only their offense but also their harm. Society will pressure you to water down your language, to make it more palatable for the favored ones. Do not dilute your medicine. Your medicine is Truth.

When you find yourself in the desert dying of thirst, run to water. Do not run away from it. You would think we would go to what is good for us. But when we are used to life and people being hurtful, we can develop an ironic attachment, a trust in hurtfulness. This trust can cause us to run from kindness, goodness, Love, and sincerity. If this is you, it is never too late to repair your compass. Do not run toward what you know even if it includes language and stories that desecrate and dehumanize you. Run toward what cures you. Sacred words and stories. Be a medicine seeker. Be careful not to dwell in cynicism. It is a trash dump that rots your soul. Dwell in Love. It is a far better garden.

Take good care of your words. They will gather your words as kindling and use them to build a fire. They will use that fire to incinerate your revolution. And to justify their supremacy and enslavement of your people. They will say it is your own words that give them the right and prove their point.

Faithfully weed out your oppressor's words and language from your own. Like picking stones from black eyed peas, or invasive plants from your garden. Their language will grow inside your revolution and poison it. Their language will be a Trojan horse inserting their spirit and ideas of you, inside your people, inside your sacred spaces. You will think you are using your own language to move out of slavery, but it will be their desecration language holding you in.

The fear in you is generations old.
Be the generation to set it free.
Be the freedom generation.
Choose new stories.

Language caught in group labels can enslave us to the plantation of group identity. The slavery virus does not care about groups, social boundaries, or borders. It cares about finding hosts, organisms that offer the right inner conditions. Create language that destroys fear.

Are you sure, dear soul, that the story you've been
telling yourself all your life is setting you free?

Life travels in circles. So should our stories. In the cultural heritage of most people worldwide, stories are not told in straight, logical lines. They are told in the same manner as life itself unfolds: unpredictable, folding back on itself, reconnecting in surprising ways. This circularity allows the sacred ingredients of the past and the future to mix with our current reality, blessing us with perspective, wisdom, meaning, and purpose. If your intent is to leach these qualities from souls and society so you may control and exploit people, you force them to tell false stories in flat, linear ways. You create educational systems to uphold and insulate this kind of storytelling. You create media systems for the same. You isolate the entire population in the kind of storytelling that fixates on individual opportunities for personal gain without responsibility to anything or anyone. Then you insert imposter heroes into the center of your story. False heroes in your own image. You include imagined villains around the perimeter of your story. This is how you fortify your supremacy. And if you are a revolutionary, you destroy all of this by helping to revive soulful, circular, ancestral story in the lives and minds of everyone.

Any peoples' cultural heritage and experienced reality are valid by virtue of those peoples' existence. A people should not have to adjudicate the truth of their oppression to those who have not lived it. And yet, this is how the dynamic plays out. Stay rooted in what you know is real. Explaining yourself is a good way to get lost in the woods of other people's denial.

Words like *plantation* and *reservation* mean very different things to those who own them and their descendant kind, than they mean to those who suffered and were tortured there, and the ones who come after them. The naming of things matters. The way you name yourself and your people and places matters even more.

If your words are not rich, nourishing soup for someone's soul, it may be best not to speak them. Serve only soul food at the table of your presence in the world. And if you are going to listen to what someone shares from their heart, listen with all of you. Make it a ceremony.

Describe people as people before you indicate their social category. Social category labels dehumanize the labeler and the ones being labeled. First say, *There goes a person, a soul, a living thing.* Say this first, before you paint the portrait of the category in which you imagine them. This is how you bring life back into a lifeless human kind. Speak first of *Life* you see in a person. Resurrection tongue.

Do not let others use their oppression language on you. The word *minority* is a violent tactic. You will never be minor. They will never be major. The only minority are those who cannot coexist in harmony as human beings and living things. Words like *underdeveloped, third world, foreign, immigrant, and illegal* can be strategic slurs intended to dehumanize and position certain groups within a caste system. Castes are by nature hostile, traumatizing, and dehumanizing. Take great care in what you call those who are unfavored. Especially if you and yours are unfavored. Your conditioning may make your language a cage. They will call your first world the third world when they are the youngest world in relation to the ancestral world of your people. Remember who you are.

When you are oppressed, you find yourself buried under certain soils: Exhaustion. Fear. Doubt. Mutedness. Dire imagination. Incarcerated pain. Dream abandonment. Relational isolation. False names. Spiritual bleaching. Abandonment of permission. Ancestral distancing. Time imprisonment. Songlessness. These are among the heavier soils. To taste sky again, you need a determination to excavate your soul. You need tools for dirt removal, and plentiful water for cleansing. Boundaries to prevent reburial. And you need new names. Oh, how you need new names.

Give yourself beautiful sacred names each day. No need to restrict yourself. There are no rules in this. Claim the ones that make your soul sigh. Each name evokes a unique part of you. Particular notes in your song. Open the windows inside you. Let yourself out. Maybe we on earth aren't lacking self-Love. Maybe we lack sacred names. Self-Love lives in the names we call ourselves, and in the names we allow ourselves to be called. Time for a whole new language. One we can whisper in the hard moments to soften the soil. One we can lullaby ourselves to sleep with at night. Endless names exist whose sound and spirit feel good to your soul, for they are native to your soul. Claim them. Watch your life become a feel good thing.

The story you tell yourself about who you are is woven of a thousand threads of repetition. To heal and be free, unravel each thread patiently. Just as patiently, weave the truth of your beautiful soul. Reweave you. Your idea of you, and therefore your life, is not an unchangeable stone. It is a weaving of rivers. A water that wants you to find the wonder in its waves. You are a creatable thing. Don't be afraid of the notes freedom sings.

Resurrect your ancestors' tongues. They are guiding you in their language. If you are not fluent in moon, moonlight cannot lead you across the meadows of night. Grow fluent in your ancestral voices. They will guide you home to freedom.

Culturally isolated, stigmatized people live in the vortex of conflict between what they are and what society expects them to be. This brings daily peril and bruising, a haunting hailstorm with shelter too rarely found. Keep alive the ancestral, generational chain of custody for your cultural truths. This is the work.

If you want to spark others on their freedom path, encourage their creative self-expression. Creativity is how the spirit reintroduces itself to the conscious mind. It is a way for the spirit to say, *Whatever you thought you were was a dream. I am your reality. I am as true and able and worthy as I say I am.*

Slaves do not believe they are worthy of happiness. Slave masters do not believe they deserve discomfort. Both statuses depend on false beliefs. Fairytales live in the heart of oppression. Sacred stories are the key to the persistent cage. Gather your storytellers, your stories, and talk story until you feel new life in you. Build your new society around these legends. Devote yourselves to never losing hold of your stories again.

The conflict within our souls regarding oppression is itself a recognition spark. A sign that we, as living things, are obligated to repair what we have wounded. What we have disordered unnaturally. Who will testify? Who will bear witness? You cannot heal a thing without the story of its harm being passed around like honored cups of tea.

Words are living things. They must be fed. Can be medicine if you choose them well. Words are the carriers of your revolution ideas. Invest in them. Bless them with long massages. Warm baths. Help them be at their best. They have so much work to do.

What you tell yourself in the worst of times
becomes your mantra in the best of times.

Reality isn't your biggest threat. Your inner stories about reality are. People say, *I have trouble sleeping.* What they really mean is, *I have trouble storying.* Our story creates our condition. The best time to examine, mend, and reweave your stories is all the time. Do it when you are awake, so you dream better in your sleep. Do it when you sleep, so you live better when you are awake. When life grows daunting, sit with your stories and spend special time. If you neglect your stories, they fray and turn against you. If you nurture your stories, they will carry you through the worst and bring you all the way to a paradise called *Peace* in a land called *Freedom.* We are not only living through the season of our circumstances. We are journeying through our stories. Our healthy stories are water in the desert. *Drink.* Hope in the valley. *Graze.* Mountains in the mist. *Climb.* Medicine for our memory. *Pour.* Manna for the masses. *Share all the food. Let your people feast.*

CHILDREN AND FREEDOM

Those who oppress you learn their oppression tactics as children. They hear their parents and other adults speak myths and fables that uphold the rightfulness of their supremacy and the subhuman quality of their inferiors. These children listen. They see the stories come to life in the world. They see the affirmation of the stories. The stories grow as seeds in them. Become part of their bodies, brains, and nervous systems. Nobody ever monitors or scans them for this foul fertility of seeds. No one ever says, *You have a disease growing in you that can end the world. Let's cure it.* One day, the child, on the way to becoming an adult, feels threatened by a world of inferiors. Magically, yet not magically at all, the old stories come out, this time from the new generation. The child of oppressors has become an oppressor. To raise free souls, we feed them freedom stories. Not only of their freedom. The freedom of all their relations, of all living things.

Your children have eyes. If you don't explain how people arrive into material poverty, your children will deduce for themselves the inferiority of impoverished people. If you don't explain achievement gaps, they will deduce unintelligence as the cause. If you don't explain the true cause of the absence of unfavored people from spaces of status, your children will deduce unworthiness as the cause. Oppression lives on attribution and deduction. On the stories by which people explain social patterns. Kill false stories of supremacy and inferiority, and what remains enlightens children to the social engineering behind social patterns. You help your young ones see.

By not immersing your children in the viral truth of oppression and caste systems, you raise adults filled with poisoned ideas of themselves, their kind, and others. The most painful thing you may have to do with your children is saturate them in truth. Because doing so means you saturate yourself in truth. You have been living in supremacy lie much longer than they have. For you to take this bath of truth is like scalding your skin in boiling water. And yet. To raise free children and not oppressors, you have no choice. Take this bath.

If you are socially favored, explain to your children why you live in a community of favored people, socialize essentially with favored people, seem to care most about the lives of favored people, are most comfortable around favored people, but insist on calling yourself blind to the traits that create favor. Explain your bitterness toward unfavored people. Why you criticize unfavored people while bowing down to favored people. Why you say favored traits don't matter though your every attitude is dictated by traits of favoring. Explain this sickness so your children develop a capacity to cure their own sickness and achieve wellness along their way.

If your children are unfavored, make sure the adults in whatever system that is supposed to serve your children actually Love your children. Do not accept them tolerating your children. Tolerance is a passive hostility. A dishonest embrace. Latent violence runs in that stream. If they in the schools and the programs and the worship centers and the hospitals and the stadiums do not Love your children, they are hurting your children and your children are hurting. Only when children feel safe can they heal and grow, open and relax, reveal and discover. Only then can your children tap the sparkling river of brilliance and giftedness running through them, descended from an elated ancestral spring. And if you say, *But I have nowhere else to place my children*, make sure you have exhausted your looking. And if you have looked and have not found, it may be time and calling for you to create those spaces where your children, with their bodies and styles, hearts and minds, hair and skin, movement and sound, energy and essence, and passions and causes, are truly Loved.

Children sit daily in the classroom of our own pain and healing, taking notes in their soul on how we behave. This role modeling we do, whether neglectful or nourishing, is how we decide the future.

The younger humans are, the more they are able to see the soul of others and stay free of supremacy. The more they are able to see their own souls. Protect their pristine vision. Your work is also to resurrect, preserve, and nurture the child spirit and vision in you.

When a soulless culture teaches children about a soulful thing, like poetry or revolution or their own heritage, the subject loses its soul as it is ingested by the children. The children then lose or never find their passion for the subject. They are left to discover the thing later in life, in their own soulful way. When they do, they fall in Love. Like they should have been able to the first time. For they are falling in Love with themselves. With life entire.

To allow your children to be daily assaulted by hate and oppression and not defend them within their relationship with you is not only to neglect them. It is an actual violence against them. A betrayal of bonds.

If you wish to kill the spirit of a people, feed them an education of stories that render them caricatures and cartoons at the farthest orbit away from the sun of your superior savior self. If you wish for the revival of the spirit of a people, honor their feeding of themselves. Honor the food of their own truth.

Negative group associations that we teach children become prisons that torture them in a personal enslavement of hate, hubris, and harm their entire lives. We raise our monsters. They don't appear magically from the mist.

Teach your children that they are born *for* their people, not *from* their people. Being born *for* their people seeds a sense of responsibility to think, act, and invest their gifts and callings toward the greater good of their people. Duty can be instilled this way, from the beginning of a life. We raise revolutionaries from birth by the way we shape how they see the world, themselves, and life. Children grow hopeless when we do not feed them hope. Without purpose when we do not feed them purpose. They are born with a fire they may not understand. Show them the forest of oppression and say, *Go, child. Burn and set us free.*

SOCIAL AND SYSTEM CHANGE

Some revolutions alter the laws and physical structures of oppression. Rarely do revolutions remove the sickness that manifested as the original and ongoing laws, systems, boundaries, and ways. Your revolution can learn to be a healer. It can treat the wound.

The most likely person to pressure someone to behave as a slave is another slave. The person most likely to pressure someone to behave as a slave master is another slave master. Peer pressure is vital in a supremacy society. Treat the elements of social conformity and you give your revolution a greater chance.

Public compliance to freedom-oriented laws will not equate to private embrace of the spirit of those laws, unless the sickness itself has been treated. For a culture to be well, it looks deep inside itself, even painfully, and treats as sacred the truth that arises, no matter how painful.

We are part of geological time. Not realizing this, we misinterpret the meaning of societies rising and falling. We believe those that rise, and their favored kind, must be superior or they would not have risen. We believe those that fall, and their unfavored kind, must be inferior or they would not have fallen. If we could see geological time clearly, we would see mountains, valleys, oceans, deserts, and forests, all rising and falling. Not due to superiority or inferiority, but to the wave dynamics of matter over time. Societies are composed of matter. Rising only happens because of falling. The reverse is true as well. Ocean peaks and troughs are children of the same sea. Rising is not fortune. Often it is precursor to sorrow. Falling is not misfortune. Often it precedes humbled fruitfulness. Landscapes are the drapery of energy, which is wild and temporal. Landscapes change. The natural world is not so impressed by rising. It knows the way of waves.

Everyone wants to arrive to freedom.
Few want to go on the journey.

You join a group to work toward freedom. Suddenly you find yourself being oppressed by its members or leaders. Your groups won't save you, won't set you free. Only your soul work can do that.

When a volcano is ready to erupt, it does not consult or defer to the wind conditions. When the time for change comes, it will not matter if your life conditions are ideal. Change is a spirit that moves when it is ready. Not when you are.

They may say, *But the social order has been this way a thousand years. It must be the way things are meant to be. There is no hope for change.* Freedom does not consider tenure or time. If an ancient tree has to die to release freedom, it dies. Freedom claims its life.

A society is not a sudden happening.
It is an ancient, hardened sediment of ideas.

If in your revolution you utilize your oppressor's ways, methods, language, spaces, habits, and measurements, you will not have a revolution. You will have a repetition. Of oppression. Many people are comfortable inside an oppressive way of life. They feel it suits and serves them. These people will resist you. Do not assume they believe anything is wrong at all. They may say they want revolution but insist that you use the oppressor's old ways. Ensure you are moving into new light together, not finding false light inside old shade.

When a small business becomes popular, large corporations want to buy it, own it. When your revolution grows popular, your oppressor will want to buy it, own it. They will seduce you with all they can think of. Stay rooted in what they are not equipped to think of: Sacredness. Sovereignty. Love. Ancestor soul. Do not be bought. Do not be sold.

Systems are always proclaiming their devotion to change: changing themselves, changing the world. But if you examine systems closely, if you autopsy the malaise in their cultural spirit, you often will find that systems spend most of their energy and focus not on change but on staying the same. They are beholden to the world that created them.

Systems created, evolved, maintained, and led by souls overrun with oppression virus are not destined to become freedom ships. Their purpose and essential nature are to perpetuate status quo. So many lifetimes have been given and lost trying to change these systems. Incremental change occurs over decades, which often is no more than dressing that better hides oppression ways. Supremacy is a dire condition. Freedom requires brave letting go and drastic rebirthing. Sometimes a people need to abandon old systems and be courageous enough to create anew their ancient, earth culture ways. Archeologists dig up artifacts and proclaim history. Revolutionaries resurrect ancestral ways and proclaim life.

Funding is how your oppressor purchases and kills off your revolution. Grants, scholarships, and donations will be offered in the name of your revolution. Each will come with obligations. The funding relief you feel will soon be followed by the familiar feeling that you are once again being owned. Careful with these seductions.

Souls drunk on supremacy are liable to ride the nowhere wave of mutated *me-ness* and status and false power until it crashes them into oblivion. They are the ones who promote projects and programs and initiatives for the people, but never stop fearing the people, devaluing the people. The ones who avoid reckoning with the people, breaking bread and truth with the people. They are not of the people, nor for the people. They lose themselves using and fleeing the people. If you want to know who truly wants people to be free, look for the ones who go beyond public protest. Who give their lives to relationship. Relationship with those who suffer. Relationship with suffering. Relationship with the medicine of Sacredness.

People with clarified self-ideas, as ordained by their own spirit and purpose, rather than by the cultural values of their oppressor, have the intangible tools and material to build healthy individual systems. For a society to be new, its systems need to be new. Not slightly altered. New. New in spirit. New in leadership. New in physical nature. New in language, values, and ways. New.

If a nation wishes to build itself, strengthen itself, heal itself, and construct a true national stability and security, it will inconvenience itself into new social norms, those psychological overseers of change. A wise nation recognizes that its strengths do not protect it from its vulnerabilities. And that how its people treat one another is its greatest vulnerability of all. Laws cannot heal this virus. Only ardent Love can do that work.

Your path is not to convince the rabid you are their equal. A rabid thing cannot fathom equality. It is lost in a fever of eating the world. Eating itself most of all. Turn away from the rabid and pour your medicine into what you Love. Into what Loves you.

Systems are powerful because they are concentrated gathering places for idea repetition, idea dissemination, idea broadcasting. Systems are the greatest polluters of collective ideas. Of cultural beliefs. They can also be potent cleansers of the polluted air, earth, and water of social ideas. Systems are filtration centers. What they filter out and into a social ecosystem determines whether they serve oppression or freedom.

It can be fruitless to be concerned about receiving justice from oppressors. They will never be driven by justice. That would be like hoping for gentleness from a hurricane. Be concerned about freedom. If your kind are free, that will be your justice.

Many say society's systems are broken. But systems do precisely what they were designed to do: perpetuate the prevailing social order. If that reality is freedom, then mainstream systems honor human beings. If that reality is oppression, then mainstream systems oppress, perpetuate supremacy. Do not spend your precious, finite life force trying to convince others that systems are broken. At best, they will pretend to agree with you, pretend to want change, pretend to make efforts. Oppressors are skilled at pretending they are working against oppression. They will snare you in meetings, committees, and initiatives that spin in circles, repeating the same conversations for decades. Centuries. Their pretending will allow time for their supremacy reign to continue. This is a stall tactic. Do not tie your revolution to pretenders or pretension. Anchor it in devotion proven through undeniable soul. Systems don't break. They reflect what is whole or broken in the culture that upholds them.

You cannot only pass new laws. You must kill the spirit that created the old laws. Otherwise your new laws are your old laws in new clothes. You cannot radiate or chemically poison this supremacy virus. It *is* radiation. It *is* poison. It will burrow, insulate, mutate, wait. When conditions are favorable it will reemerge, stronger, bolder. Kill the ailing spirit, which is the condition. The organism itself will be new. Kill the collective climate, the air of extreme individuality and conquering culture. Kill the values of greed and destruction. Kill the linearity. Resurrect the circle. Make visible the ancestors. So they may make visible our original code for being alive.

The end contains a beginning.
Have hope.

The thing about change is that it changes. Whatever you are going through is already ending. Whatever is painfully ending is already birthing a beginning. There is no end to your beginnings.

Do you feel safe in the spaces you occupy each day? Do you feel safe to use your native language? Safe to live out your customs and ways? Safe to laugh and cry as you are compelled? Safe to say no? Safe to say yes? Does your body show that you feel safe? Does it breathe? Or is it a holding place for tension, closed and protective and aching? As you assess your sense of safety, you gain a sense of your freedom or lack of it. Your revolution needs measuring sticks. Gather with your people and determine how safe you are.

Societies will heal only when they realize there is but one society: *Life*. Only when the illusory, possessive scales of territory fall away, and humans see there is only Creation, interdependent and trembling with fragility. Only then.

Educational systems in oppressive societies exist primarily to transmit cultural values, not to objectively teach Truth. This directive fixates on transmitting the glory story of the oppressor, and on keeping out the human story of the oppressed. This is true for all systems under oppression climate.

If you are a student, make sure your teacher Loves or hates you. Your most valuable lessons arrive that way. You are always a student.

Education without continuous student autobiography, storytelling, is not education. It is colonization of the mind. Testimonial storytelling broadcasts our humanity, reminding ourselves and others of our sacred worth. When the student speaks, and the teacher learns, now you have education.

Slaves sing plantation lullabies, lulling themselves to sleep with a dependent mentality. One that says they need society to grant them their humanity and full participation in life. But enslaved souls are their own grantor. Liberation is in their hands. To be free, a people must choose new songs.

Systems do not change because those who control them change. Centuries and millennia of history testify to this. Systems change when oppressed communities change themselves and the way in which they participate in those systems.

Certain soil does not grow sacredness. Whatever seeds you sow, it desecrates. Rots into its own essence. Know what ground you are gardening. Sometimes it is necessary to move on to the next plot of land.

Beware of those who want to put you in charge. They don't always want you to be a master. Sometimes they want you to be a slave.

Letting people through the doors without changing what is behind the door is not diversity or any other rhetorical word. It is tokenism. Perpetuation of supremacy in secluded spaces. For true progress, cleanse the spaces. Fumigate. Renovate.

Assimilation is a word oppressors use to say, *Come, let us swallow you alive.* Assimilation is genocide. You can honor the benevolence in any space, culture, or country, and still be you. You should never have to dissolve who you are into the image of your oppressor as a condition of freedom. Do not live for their approval. Live to honor your ancestors. Keep your name, language, accent, skin, hair, faith, stories, ways. Keep your soul. Keep your life.

Poisons can be diverse. Malice and murder can be diverse. *Diversity* is not intrinsically beneficial. Work toward diversity of wellness, diversity of genius, diversity of freedom expression. Diversifying spaces means nothing if those spaces continue to serve the supremacy status of some, and the oppression of others.

Diversity, equity, and *inclusion* are often no more than hostile forms of tokenism, assimilation, erasure, and genocide, unless the membership, leadership, and spaces involved purge themselves of supremacy, antipathy, and oppression. What does it matter if your space is diverse if it is in the image and culture of the oppressor? What does it matter if your space is equitable if it is equitable under the terms and conditions of the oppressor? What does it matter if your space is inclusive if everyone included must hew to the sensitivities, values, and ways of the oppressor? Do not fall for these oppression tactics. They are slick and long practiced, and serve only the status quo. Marginalized people do not need to be fixed, cured, improved, to *qualify* for inclusion. Those who harbor and host supremacy and oppression sickness need to cure and evolve themselves, along with the spaces they control. So that these spaces are not only safe, but also in the image, spirit, and culture of all who inhabit them. Be not impressed with an invitation to join a space if the space is polluted with dehumanizing spirit and ways, and void of soul and life. As with all invitations, before you commit, find out what kind of party is going down.

Do not accept honorary membership among slave masters. They will always see you as a slave. Honorary membership confers certain privileges, but the fine print is always hidden and blisters you when you are touched by its conditions. Honorary membership brings you closer into their spaces so they can get you drunk on their wine of false acceptance, then parade you as evidence of their hospitality.

Believing in equality does not make a person a liberator. It does not absolve that person of being an oppressor. *Equality* is a vague convenience of language. Nobody can pin it down in the phenomenal world. Focus on equality tends to serve the oppressor, who does not believe in equality. If you want to be a liberator, focus on the purging of your own soul. Cleanse your being of false and degrading ideas of others, of yourself. When your own soul is clarified, now you are a liberator.

Your oppressors will offer you their physical spaces in which to gather for your revolution. They will offer you their technology, their materials, their food and drink, their communications outlets. They will offer you everything. This way they can own your revolution and continue to own you. They know if you grow dependent on their resources, your revolution will be at their mercy. They will grind it to dust.

How can a frightened orchard produce a courageous fruit? Leaders grow from the same soil and garden or desolation that the people do. Our leaders are nothing more than a reflection of ourselves, the masses. Leaders don't just pop up, they are raised up. By the masses. The values and characteristics of our leaders are no more than the values and characteristics of the society they come to lead. Leaders are mirrors of our own condition. If our leaders fail us, it is because we have already failed ourselves. Freedom work is not about choosing better leaders. It is about healing the garden from which leaders grow.

In slave societies, institutions ultimately serve the status quo, the oppressive arrangement, the viral idea of supremacy and inferiority. No matter their propaganda or self-delusion, institutions are seduced into serving the prevailing, dominant spirit of their society. If they do not, they are targeted, assailed, and often die. For an institution to be rebellious against a sickened slavery society, its entirety needs passionate wellness. From its groundwater, soil, roots, foundation, structure, and atmosphere, to its energy, spirit, and aura, it depends on passionate devotion to being well. Wellness allows an institution to withstand the barrage of a nation outraged that it would dare to resist oppression culture.

Pay close attention to where you are accepted and where you are not. Oppression herds your kind like cattle into the spaces that serve its cause, not your dignity. You may come to believe that certain spaces are made for you, because all you have known is seeing your kind in those spaces. Prisons can be called many other things to make those spaces more appealing. They are still prisons. Incarceration is a favored dumping ground in the appetite of those sick on supremacy.

Freedom requires collective cleansing of the heart. Law changes are crucial, but changes of the heart are essential. Self-reckoning is the method: *What is my place in the sacred web of life, in the scheme of humanity? For what am I responsible?*

Desegregation involves the removal of laws and physical structures that separate groups. The idea that exposing people to each other creates harmony is wishful. The conditions under which people interact determine the outcome of those interactions. Social exposure under oppressive conditions only solidifies supremacy codes. Integration is another concept oppressors use to serve their status quo. In your revolution, ask, *Into what are we integrating? Why would we want to integrate with anything that dehumanizes us?* Examine whether you are participating in symbiosis or being consumed. Stay on the path that purifies and alters the soul of souls.

Sacred union is an emotional and spiritual acceptance, development of respect, and appreciation for an outcast group. An honest reckoning with the inhumanity one's own group and oneself have heaped upon others who are fully human. A painful, tearing, self-shaming, soul-searching, humbling acquiescence to the truth of what oppressor attitudes have wrought globally. And to the truth that one is responsible by inheritance for the unjust nature of society. Personal responsibility is always the heart of revolution and social healing. Individuals are the carriers of generational transmission. This work is born, lives, and endures in the person.

The dire need to be at the top, in the center, controlling all things, leading the way, being the ultimate authority is literally a sociopathic condition. A pathology in the social sense. Do not let this pathology have its way. Hold your center. Hold yourselves in your center.

Caste systems are never dismantled by the beneficiaries. Generations of caste reality leave them feeling deeply entitled to not only their station, but also to the comfort of having others beneath them, indentured to them, affirming and praising them. Without these security blankets, their nights would be too cold, their days too exposed and vulnerable. It is left to those already cold, exposed, and vulnerable to will revolution. If their pain is terrible enough, they have a chance to overcome their comforts and fears to destroy the structure to which all casted souls are accustomed.

To focus on harmony between groups in an oppressive, supremacist society that serves the favored group while destroying the others is to uphold the unnatural order of that society. Oppression has many ploys. This is one of them. True harmony is the offspring of sincere societal efforts to honor the sacredness of every soul. Only in a just society can true harmony exist. Without sacredness toward all, harmony between all is no more than a distraction tactic. Distraction is one of the most potent threats to revolution. Remain centered in your endeavor.

Truth and reconciliation is not just the name of a program, process, or strategy. It is the energetic nature of healing. Introduce the medicine of Truth directly into the viral sickness. Create conditions in which this truth medicine reconciles fragmented, separated, traumatized parts within the organic body. In society, true healing requires much more than desegregation, which is the changing of laws. It requires a changing of the heart. Of the mind. Of the collective soul that tethers people to the sickness of inferiority and superiority. It requires getting down on hands and knees and opening up the torrent of emotions from within. Expelling the ailment itself. This is the great humbling. The cry for forgiveness. Healing is the core of rightful empowerment. For how can you have, hold, and exercise sacred power if your center is in pieces? How can you be sacred power if you exude woundedness?

Less training.
More healing and growing.

You cannot train prejudice and supremacy out of people. This is a spiritual matter. A sickness of the soul. Only the infected can save themselves. What they have become must be willing to die if they are to have any hope of letting their true soul live. Freedom work requires less training and more healing. Less thinking and more feeling. Less memorizing and more remembering. Less formality and more wild abandon. Less linearity and more circularity. Less hierarchy and more anarchy. Less droning and more drumming. Less song and dance and more sacred dance and song. Less policy and more passion. Less authority and more ancestry. Less sound and more silence. Less professionalism and more soulfulness. An entire, beautiful mess.

Concrete tools mean nothing in the hands of someone in a concrete condition. It takes fluidity, pliability, flexibility, softness, and permeability to learn, grow, heal, and be a miracle of change. People come to you for teaching, *guruing*, and guidance. They say, *Give us some concrete tools.* In response, you say, *You are the concrete tool. And that is the problem. You cannot solve suffering with concrete. I have come to set you afire. That your hardness be softened, made fluid and flowing, a magma of Grace. That your soul be set free to run rampant and do its mystic work in this world. Your answers are not outside you. They are asleep within you. To wake them, you must feel deeply. You must burn. This is what my Love flame is for.*

Do your daily work to clarify what your revolution intends to replace oppression with. What does your collective freedom look like? The world changes daily. Evolve your vision accordingly. People need to see where this freedom train is going.

When you are living in a garbage dump, you don't breathe too deeply. This is how it is living in a society polluted with hateful supremacy. Which is why everyone suffocates, and even newborns breathe with a shallowness. We need fresh new air.

Slaves on a certain plantation wanted to be free. So they ran away to a new land. They made sure to bring with them all the things they knew. Chains, shackles, whips, nooses, hatred, and cruelty. Dehumanizing ways. In their new land, soon they had created, not freedom, but their very own plantation. When you use your oppressor's tools in an attempt to get free, you end up creating just another form of slavery.

When you become what your enemy has been to you, you become your truest enemy. This is promised.

If you use your oppressor's standards of behavior and character to aspire to your people's freedom, the journey's destination will not be freedom. It will be oppression. Only you will have become an oppressor. Carrying supremacy virus is one thing. Allowing it to overrun you is another. Being favored and positioned by society to spread and weaponize the virus completes the fatal jeopardy.

If you use conquest and domination ways in your revolution, you will bury your own kind in conquest and domination. What goes forth comes back. What is poured, pours back into the pourer. Now you will be the blight upon the world.

Resist the powerful urge to appropriate what has been used against you. Go to Sacredness and ask it for its tools.

It is vital to consider what you will do when you reach freedom's mountaintop. Will you scream? Will you stay there or descend? Will you erect barriers preventing others from the summit? If so, you will lose your mountaintop. You will instantly find yourself in the desolate foothills of oppression.

It is imperative to hold internal, intrinsic soul standards for how you treat yourself and others. Standards not subject to social tides and personal moods and moons. This is how you keep your integrity, how you stay worthy of the sacred web.

YOUR RELATIONSHIPS

Some people will be offended by your freedom. Leave them to their chains. Funny how freedom changes the situation. Notice who is happy for your freedom. Ride with them. And keep sowing. Freedom conditions are founded in wellness. This is the base, the ground from which your freedom harvest grows. Rest, sleep, nutrition, exercise, movement, dance, song, drum, ceremony, gatherings, prayer, tears, memory, ancestors, elders, children, sacred relations, breathing, listening, life. What is the condition of your conditions? Tend to that.

Your family and friends believe they know you because their projected idea of you is very old. They are deeply attached to this idea. Often, their idea of you does not contain your freedom, so why work so hard to preserve their idea of you?

153

You endure so many masters in life. Don't let your Loved ones' idea of you be one of those.

When people in your life project onto you the nature of other people who have hurt them, they are not experiencing you. They are caught in a terrible dream. While you can feel empathy and compassion for them, you do not have to join them in their dream. Be true to yourself. Do not adopt the ways projected onto you. Those ways are an invasive species not native to your soul. Be true. And when you find those who see you for you, without projection, treasure them for caring enough to truly see. Those are your holy mirrors. Look into that divine glass and remember your glory everlasting.

It may be tempting to catch a ride on the back of a society-favored partner, friend, family, work, space, neighborhood, or cause. But if you are of an unfavored kind, all such rides end with you fallen, trampled, and in the dirt. Some call this ride-sharing a form of selling out, of passing. The only thing you pass into is the saddest performance art of all. The shame-soaked hiding of who you are. Be gentle, for we have all caught such fateful rides. Be good to yourself. Forgive yourself. Learn to stay off those exploitive rides. Embrace the sublime locomotion of freedom.

Who are your people? Those oppressed with you. Who are your kind? Those enslaved with you. Who are your truest people and kind? Those who will rise with you.

Those who Love you and those who want you well, even if it violates their idea of you, are not always the same people. Discerning your true kind is not easy in a parade of masks and costumes. Who wants you free? They are likely a small population compared to the bazaar of people who simply want you. Want you for what they can get from you. Make your offerings to those who care to heal and grow. Hang out in the part of the market where real produce is being shared mutually and freely. Avoid the hagglers and hasslers. Kneel down beside the quiet farmers, the ones with dirt beneath their nails.

Things will be said about you.
Be you regardless.

Nurturing yourself through a sense of aloneness and isolation is at the heart of your precious freedom work. Loss and fear of loss. Social repercussions. Comfort versus discomfort. Revolutionaries often inherit lonesomeness. It is their heritage. Spiritually, this path strips you down to your core essence. The path is not easy. Just essential. And made of Grace. Many souls are with you as you work and live for freedom. Treat the lonesomeness by holding ceremony that reminds you of this and rejoins you with your revolutionary kind.

If you want a world that reflects what you care about, invest in those who are working intimately and sacredly for the common good, because the common good is likely to include what your soul cares about. Do not trivialize those who craft and create from their sacred calling. They are a particular womb of freedom.

Are you practicing freedom in your relationships? That is the question. Your relationships are microcosms of the world. They contain every oppression the world contains. They are your proving grounds. Create rites of passage for your collective freedom work. Examine the journey of how you treat each other. Have ceremonies celebrating how you are learning Sacredness.

Train yourself for solitude. Freedom work will take you there. You can grow accustomed to its particular climate. As with all things, practice. Small doses, then larger. In time, solitude can feel like an indulgent retreat. Gestation happens in the silence and solitude of the womb. Then birth, and the whole world gets blessed. Let yourself. Heal. Create. Grow. Like this. Do not underestimate the power of solitude to fuel your freedom work, to electrify your revolution. Solitude is crucial in a freedom diet. It returns us to our Source and sustenance. It reunions us with our own soul, an affirming voice that we are on the freedom path.

If they help you get your soul right, don't run.
Take your medicine.

Be willing for your relationships to change. Breathe and release your lifestyle, habits, ideas, self-ideas, beliefs, emotional patterns, dreams, even your memories. Cultivate a passion for letting go. Foster also a vital trait in your personality: gathering into your life your sacred circle of kindred souls. They will be the web that keeps you afloat.

GOOD PEOPLE

The most powerful incubators of supremacy virus are those who are more concerned with considering themselves to be good people than with addressing the virus in them, in their lives, in their relations. Those favored by oppression are determined to believe no oppressor exists, no oppressed exist, oppression does not exist, and all such things are myths. Their entire sense of being a good person is that the social order is a reflection of the qualities of people and groups. They see no injustice in the essence of their place in the world. Of course they must be superior. How else would they have arrived to their station?

Many people believe if they have no hate in their heart, they cannot possibly be an oppressor. Oppression does not require hate. It only requires that you participate in oppression. The subtle clouds in you of supremacy and inferiority bring plenty of rain to feed the fatal forest that dehumanizes human beings.

Some people want to believe they are good people because they are not slave masters. But yet they are spouse, friend, colleague, collaborator to the master. They are enablers. They uphold slavery by valuing their relationship over their morality, over their character, over their own sacred life.

Favored people who feel they are good people in their treatment of unfavored people, yet do nothing to challenge those people's oppression or their oppressors, are the true enablers of supremacy. In their silence, avoidance, inaction, and subconscious, unreckoned prejudices, supremacy imbeds itself and remains protected and carried forward. Their souls are the soil where supremacy grows like fungus, to be tapped when necessary by the more flagrant mercenaries of hate. These good people are the incubators. They are all the hope oppressors ever need.

Oppressors are obsessed with convincing themselves they are good persons. Obsessed with convincing the world of this. Being seen as a good person is more important to them than being a good person. Far more important than healing, wellness, justice, collective benefit. The slave master virus turns souls into cannibals, narcissists, bullies, sociopaths. They literally cannot coexist with other living things. They are inflamed with a strong impulse to destroy everything.

Including themselves. They would rather die than own their illness or work to cure it.

Supremacy is not transmitted most potently from hater to hater, but from denier to denier. From enabler to enabler. From silent beneficiary to silent beneficiary. These souls who care more about being perceived as good than they care about instigating social goodness. They are the breeding ground. Their children grow up with no one explaining the perverse social order all around them. So these children conclude for themselves that some groups must simply be superior and others inferior. That everyone must deserve their social position and all the favoring or oppression that comes to them.

Once supremacy burrows into the soul of a society, only the silent beneficiaries and loud performers of goodness can purge the sickness from society by marginalizing the extreme oppressors. Yet such would-be healers must be conditioned for the healing task. This is a virus that feasts on suffering and unwellness. Pain can turn a good soul narcissistic, consumed and contorted into its suffering. This is how the virus enters, multiplies, escapes through villains, heroes, everyone.

Dislike, disbelief, devaluation, disregard, denial, discomfort, and fear are sufficient to be an oppressor. Mild aversion to unfavored people is more destructive than blatant hate. It seeps and creeps unattended like mold and mildew into the fabric of everything. Pretends to be Love.

Do you choose to see the world in a way that justifies suffering, or in a way that heals suffering? This is the moral of your life story. Your goodness has nothing to do with it.

Supremacy casts people as good or bad. Hero or villain. Civilized or savage. No dimension or texture. This way it can justify the evils of the oppressive good people as a function of their goodness, and the suffering of the oppressed bad people as a function of their badness. Simplified, unintelligent processing. This is how supremacy creates and maintains its world order. If you want a free world, be willing to think in complexities.

People will repeat robotically that they do not see the differences between peoples upon which their very supremacy is built. If they didn't see people in those terms, if they didn't notice such outward features and inward traits, they wouldn't speak so often of their blindness to those things. Their claimed blindness is their nervous mantra, as if reassuring themselves, *I am a good person. I am a good person. I am a good person.* Meanwhile their entire lives are coded to those social differences and categories. Where they live, who they socialize with, where their children go to school, where they worship, who they pay, how much they pay them. They are sad marionettes doing a denial dance, strings pulled by a disease they were raised in, with no capacity to even utter the words that describe their caste or the castes of those beneath them. They are in great pain suppressing a tide of unnatural order that will not abate its assault on their conscience. They want a way out. They are the way out. They will not take the way.

How do I and my kind benefit from being favored? A question to ask daily if you want to heal yourself of supremacy. Or if you care to heal your society and humanity. Run from this question and you pollute the world. Move into this question and become a freshwater spring.

It is not kindness to protect those infected with supremacy virus from the truth of their affliction. Don't be afraid to let a *good* person know they are unwell.

No matter how kind a person is, this does not absolve that person of their supremacy or oppression of other living things. Kindness with underlying prejudice is not kindness. It is conditional, exclusive favoritism. True kindness is a wellspring of Love, which is unconditional. Even when it does not wish to be.

The most beautifully spirited people can harbor this most ugly blight, and carry its tragic seed into the world, into generations. It is the one thing these beautiful persons cannot shake from their soul. To hate, reduce, or abuse your neighbor on earth is to destroy yourself in the heaven that is your soul.

The contradiction between the oppressive way of life people participate in and uphold, and their need to believe they are good people, creates a debilitating identity conflict. Overwhelmingly, this conflict is managed through denial and avoidance. The favored ones grow mute. Guilt boils into resentment. Hatred and rage come easily when they perceive someone is about to puncture and deflate their generational lie: the supremacy story upon which their entire sense of goodness has been constructed. To ask such people to see their complicity, to see the pathology by which they have lived, is to ask them to kill themselves and all they know. For nothing in their life is not entangled in this lie, this evil treatment of the unfavored kind, this indefensible arrogance. You are asking them to betray their kingdom. Be ready for a hellfire resistance. Stay in your peace.

Oppressors tend not to see themselves as a distinct cultural product, with lineage, spirit, and worldviews descending from ancestral values and beliefs. This benefits their oppression reign. Allows them to see themselves as normal, good people, separate and apart from the blatant supremacists and hate carriers on which their own moderate life station depends.

Do you see the oppression of others? Do you take action against the oppression of others? Do you sincerely seek out the roots of oppression in you? Do you work to heal them? Your answer to these questions is a far greater indicator of your *goodness* than are the stories you tell yourself about your goodness. Assess your soul.

EARTH CULTURES AND CONQUEST CULTURES

Humankind can be understood as people existing in earth ways and cultures, and conquest ways and cultures. Conquest cultures may lead to material acquisition, but certainly doom their descendants to an eventual suffering of natural imbalance and obstructed flow in the soul. Their people are ultimately conquered by their conquering.

Earth cultures may be of meager material means, though they are wealthy in their relation to all living things. A river of spirit, wellness, balance, and vitality flows through their people. Their ways are sustainable and tend toward healing. Earth cultures and conquest cultures exist on far opposite ends of the same spectrum. Most cultures throughout history fall somewhere in between.

Human beings are indigenous living things, no matter how we forget this truth. Indigenous to earth. Indigenous to a way of surviving and thriving on earth. Our original, indigenous directive includes this: *Act as a group. Act as a group to heal, create, grow, nurture, reconcile, build, imagine. Act as a group to live in a beautiful, sacred way.*

Humanhood is not a birthright. It is an achievement of painful healing and growth. If you are able to relate to yourself, others, and all living things in an honoring way, we shall call you human. In supremacy societies, humanhood is granted sparse weight or value. Humanhood threatens supremacy societies. It is a constant vibrational hum that says to such nations, *You are now violating Humanhood. Everything about your way of life violates this sacred code.*

Souls infused with freedom spirit seek harmony for the world. Souls saturated in supremacy virus seek control over the world. They are ponderous boulders perched on cracking ice coating lakes of illusion. They know at any moment the ice will give way and they will plunge to their fate. The fate of falsity.

Original, ancestral, indigenous human values for sharing carried an expectation that those who have will give, give to enrich the common good. The code for life is written in a key of mutuality. Your revolution cannot escape this verse.

Inside this contemporary, individualistic world, the concept of *interdependence* has become misunderstood, even perverted. What was once a natural reflex in its original context is now seen as evidence of sloth, dependency, selfishness. In the intimate communal web that birthed our enduring traits, dependency was a beautiful and required thing. When all are dependent on each other, dependency sings into a wholeness that works for everyone. Only in a world of hoarding, territoriality, possessiveness, and worship of the material over the relational, is dependency a sinful banging of the keys.

Societies whose people strain to escape one another rather than find relationship with each other reveal a collective spiritual immaturity. A deficit of soul and consciousness. This is a sure reflection of greed culture values and a loss of earth culture ways. An honest examination of our relational anxiety leads to a useful diagnosis and prescription: We need our relational ancestral ways.

Oppressive, individualistic cultures take all that they can, for as long as they can, until the world is dead and empty. They do not care what this will mean for future generations, or even for their own children. They are consumed in a fever of the self, a fever of the now. They believe past and future do not exist, do not matter. They have contorted an old, earth cultures truth about the present into an unrecognizable idea of selfishness that justifies and suits the way they abuse and dishonor both the past and the present. They follow false prophets who themselves stole the original earth cultures truths and presented them as their own.

Earth cultures are not ingrained to act without deeply caring consideration of how they are touching the past and the future alive inside their present. Believe your soul when it says to you that all of time is a circle, all happenings are happening now, in you. You touch all of it. Are touched by all of it. Honor and learn from what has been and what will be. All of it already *is*. Care-take this sacred land we call eternity.

Earth cultures share kinship systems that are freedom's fabric. We cannot be disconnected, isolated, and hyper individualized and experience freedom. Freedom is a totality. A communion and oneness that frightens individualistic, materialistic souls and cultures. Freedom is the decadence of being together.

Say these words:
I am not a person. I am a people.
Earth is my soul.

Earth soil is not your only sovereign land. Your kinship circle is sovereign land. Your sacred gatherings are sovereign land. Your memories are sovereign land. Your ancestors are sovereign land. Your ancestral ways are sovereign land. Your wellness is sovereign land. Do not believe you are a homeless people. You are full of home. This makes you free.

Maybe you are crossing a stretch of grass. Looking down you see worms and ants doing what they do. Maybe you are tempted to feel superior to those small, distant creatures who exist in a way that seems so foreign to you. Maybe you feel they are invaders, invalid immigrants into your life. Maybe you feel a violence surge up in you, an impulse to destroy what is vulnerable to your particular power. Maybe to justify your destruction lust you weave story in your mind of the inferiority of these little things at your feet. Maybe one day you die and your body, once so large in comparison, now is the dust on the blades of grass. And the worms and ants, those little things, are not to you so little anymore. Maybe your entire life you were dreaming of being bigger and more important than the world, and your fear held you in that orbit, that false nightmare of separation and combat. Maybe you have not yet died, and, still full of the breath of life, you have a chance to change your way of seeing and feeling things. Maybe today you sit on the grass in serenity and join the worms and the ants in the harmony of living things.

HISTORY AND HEALING

Until you identify ground zero in an epidemic or pandemic, you cannot understand the source, the pathogen, or the mode of transmission. This is why history matters in overcoming supremacy, oppression, and colonizing, generational social conditioning. The plague was birthed somewhere, in some people, within a specific petri dish of culture. Locate those people. Understand their condition. Crack the code of this virus as it mutates and spreads. Create counterculture conditions in your life spaces. Immunize your people. Strengthen your ceremonies for pouring story of heritage, healing, and wellness between generations. Historical awareness is an inhospitable climate for supremacy-inferiority virus. It cannot survive in souls who know who they truly are.

All peoples have a sacred culture, authentic to their history and heritage of Love and honor within their circle. All peoples have a desecrated culture, which is not their true culture at all. Desecrated culture is the distorted, polluted artifact of a people's unwellness. It often becomes popularized as an ingrained, imagined idea of who a people are. Their rumored type and way. Anyone who cares to know a people's sacred culture will make the effort to know their history and heritage. The record is always available in the stories they share.

Yesterday makes Love to today so that
today may give birth to tomorrow.

History is a living thing. A breathing species of Love and generations. The circle of life is everything. History is not facts. It is the essential river of life. If you do not swim in this water you cannot truly say you are living.

Freedom work is most fertile when rooted in heritage, the actual journey of a people. Freedom workers do not allow their labor to be a tourist's gaze into something forged as foreign, as cold ideas. Their mother's kitchen brewed the tonic they now drink. Their ears heard history directly from their grandmothers' and grandfathers' mouths. They wore it as children in the cold. They splashed around naked in it in childhood summer heat. It was the mud they wore as cloth. This history was the music, stories, warnings, fables, ways, quirks, artifacts, haunts, personalities of their adornment. Then these freedom workers grew up, walked straight into the trees, and with their bare hands gathered the rest of what had been left behind, stolen, buried, burned, discredited, washed away, distorted. Now they bring it all back to us. Freedom workers return to us, wet and gleaming, our own supple sap and naked nectar.

A free child can say to herself of others: *These people are a limb of my very own humanity that utterly reverberates across the ages, announcing itself on the shores of my limb of humanity. These people are a window into the deeper meaning of my people. These people are actually and fully people, therefore sacred things.*

Over generations, or even over a lifetime, slaves can come to believe their way of being is their original culture, when in truth their current way of being is a reproduction of the favored culture. Straining out our own cultural ways from the ways of our oppressor is vital labor. Unavoidable reckoning. Liberating souls assert their own truth and reality, their own humanity, without wearing the cloak of living in the image of their oppressor.

Culture is a people's way of being. It is their entire fabric, regardless of the category to which they are assigned. To try to reduce culture to one dimension is to reduce humans to less than human. This is how the concept of culture goes from being freedom song to genocidal tool.

Our flighty, lazy, habitual rehashing of the same historical revolutionary figures renders them as tokens, separate from the masses they existed within during their lifetimes. This syrupy, one-dimensional stroking does very little to penetrate the tissue of deep-rooted prejudice, mythology, and dehumanized ideas. It does very little to explain to our children why they exist in and inherit an oppressive world. This explanation is necessary so our children have a fair opportunity to deduce the reason certain people occupy the top social rung and certain other people occupy the rung that in countless ways sinks farther into the mud. So they can judge the validity of rungs in the first place. If we do not give our children this history and create the context for today's inequities, they are vulnerable to concluding what has always been concluded in the private hearts of many: *Those people are down there because they are inferior. And those people are up there because they are superior. And generational inheritance means nothing in this equation because after all, we are a free society in which anyone can be anything they want.* This is the cold, deceiving psychology of attribution. Of cause and blame. Our responsibility with regard to history and heritage is to *tell our children the story*, even as it journeys through the darkness of collective shame. This is how the sun is enticed to rise.

Supremacist oppression requires and breeds pathological dishonesty in favored persons, to help them reason the nature of their existence. This dishonesty concentrates itself in increasing toxicity with each passing generation. Until they cannot tell the story of their history without lying obscenely. Until they cannot bear the true story of any people, including their own.

Telling the history of a people is not a favor to those people. It is a favor to the organism that is a society. Bearing witness heals fragmented, desecrated nations, communities, families, and souls. True history is a favor to the favored, allowing them to gain a corrected perspective of their proportionate value in this world. It gives them a glimpse into their true, humbled place in the sacred web.

As long as we examine a people outside of the context of their root heritage we are doing nothing more than bouncing beach balls beside a hungry tide. Before we can say we know a family, we have to go beyond playing with the children. We have to introduce ourselves to the parents, politely receive the grandparents, and break bread with the generational family narrative. We have to spend time with the entire personality and whole story. This is how we come to know a people.

If they do not know your people's human history, do not trust that they see your people as fully human. Especially if they seem prideful in claiming to not see differences. This is their way of running from their fear of and discomfort with your people. As if to say, *I will imagine you and your people as an honorary version of my people who are the favored kind. I will imagine your inferiority away, so that I may call myself a good person and not be haunted by guilt in my sleep.*

You cannot fully respect the humanity of a people if you aren't aware of the human lives from which those people descend. Respect and honor are not that easy. Heritage is fully appreciated only when its fullness has been intimately examined, illustrated, and discoursed through generations until it becomes inherently institutional. Until it is in the foundations, walls, windows, ducts, and ceilings of schools and homes. And resides in the electrical waves of media transmission. This kind of century-by-century adherence to examination and celebration is what creates value for the subject in the hearts of children and adults. We have not even begun to reach the river's other side when it comes to creating heart value for historically oppressed human beings.

CONSIDERING VIOLENCE

If you stand for freedom, peace, Love, they will call you violent. They will convict you and nail you to a cross. *Violent* is a word they use to contain you. To quell your fire. When they call you violent what they really mean is: *You feel threatening to our arrangement. So threatening that we feel like doing violence. Violence is all we know. The only lens we can see through is the violence of abusive power and control. Because we feel so much violence when we think of you, see you, hear you, you must be violent. You haunt us. You violate our comfort. Because of you, we have a right to violence.*

Defending your people against hate and dehumanization, whether blatant assaults or subtle erosion, is not the same spirit as assaulting a people for their self-defense. A righteousness courses through people willing to defend themselves from genuine oppression. A righteousness that will not be quelled.

If you communicate your revolution violently, you will destroy your message and the spirit soil in which to plant your seed. You may believe violent words and tone can set your people free. Humans and violence are like forests and fire. Some fire can bless the forest, but if the burning never ends, so will end the forest. Violent broadcasting of your revolution may propel progress in some ways, may recruit some souls. Eventually, however, if you do not offer Love's oxygen to your people, they will burn up inside the atmosphere of self-destruction, which offers no hopeful air.

If your society depends on perpetual war to exist, it is not a society. It is a war machine in which each person, civilian or military, plays their role. If what you have created requires constant defense, maybe it is the world that needs defending from what you have created. When ceaseless, invasive offense is cast as patriotic defense, the concept of patriotism is ripe for reckoning. War is not freedom, even if you believe you have won. Freedom from war is freedom. Fly that flag on every peak.

Love does not consider violence or nonviolence. Love is truly unconditional. Without condition. Not the condition of violence. Not the condition of nonviolence. Love lives beyond those dimensions. Its only law is itself. Its only restriction is itself.

What will you do as a parent to save your children?
Be that willing to save your people.

Violence and violation are not siblings. They are the same soul. If you are being violated, that is violence. While you debate using violence in your revolution, a more profound violence is being done to you. Violate that. Love for your people is more powerful than any medicine. It can penetrate any armor of malice. Love for your people does not predetermine the limits of what it will do to arrive at freedom. Moral restraints do not decide. Love decides.

While you are busy pledging nonviolence or being conflicted about violence, your oppressor will continue violating you. Here is an emotional portrait for those unfamiliar with being violently, systemically, culturally oppressed: It is like swimming in an ocean of hostility and dehumanization. Every moment. Every day. Your entire life. While being told by your oppressors, *If you don't like this ocean, then leave.*

They will say you are inciting violence. Stay rooted. You are inciting freedom. Which is Love. To those who slander your revolution as violent while upholding oppression, Truth has a response: *You are a slave master whipping slaves while you demand the slaves pledge not to be violent against the slave master. You will not divert our course with your illegitimate interrogation on violence. We will do what Love compels us to do.*

SPECIAL TREATMENT

When someone encourages you to not intervene in a human crisis, run from them. They are sick with oppression virus. When someone encourages you to not intervene in your own family's crisis, run even faster.

Your oppressor will suppress your freedom voice by saying, *We are all one, so you should focus on our oneness.* And you should. Focus on the oneness within yourself. Your oneness with the living world. Your oneness with those who honor you, respect, and care for you and your kind. You are not obligated to spend your life force merging with those who are threatened even by your oneness with yourself. Your oppressor peddles a oneness that is the oneness of a predator devouring prey. You are digested into parasitic oneness. Nothing remains of you, but your predator is full and satisfied. Your oppressor is happy for you to be consumed in this kind of oneness for centuries. Your true oneness work is Love work. It requires mutual deep caring

171

between those weaving sacred union together. This requirement causes true oneness work to separate the sheath of appearances from the raw shaft of Truth. Those whose spirit does not honor your kind will blow away in the wind of your communion labor. Those whose spirit is sincere will remain. Here is where you can grow a sacred oneness rather than merely a social, strategic one. If your freedom work with some people does not feel symbiotic to your soul, consider what you may need to shed. Be willing to shed even the bright and celebrated ones. Stay one with the sacred integrity of your soul.

Oppression creates mentalities that say, *I serve all the people, all the children*. This language is the expression of a deep discomfort with attending to the damage caused by the societal sickness of social supremacies. When people tell you all lives matter, ask them why they don't care that some of those lives are in dire trouble. Ask why they are trying to pull firefighters away from the fire.

When a house is on fire, you direct your resources to putting out the fire in that house. You don't stand back and say, *All houses matter*. You don't pretend you care about the whole neighborhood, but privately resent when repairs are made to the streets and homes most needing repair. This is an oppression tactic. It is ancient. Numerous royals have convinced their subjects to care most about the wellbeing of the royals, and that advocating for commoners was selfish and divisive. Oppression has no new tricks. Just old tools it keeps polished and ready.

When you have a hole in your boat, you do not go around saying, *I serve all of the boat*. You realize that if you do not repair the hole, your boat will sink and you will perish. You put your attention, resources, and time into repairing the hole. You don't worry about the other parts of the boat feeling neglected, as though they somehow deserve equal focus in the name of a convoluted and manipulated idea of equality, inclusion, and fairness. Mend the hole. Save the boat.

When your immune system is overwhelmed by addressing a concentrated area of breakdown in the body, its capacity to maintain or serve the rest of the system is compromised. This is how freedom work is. Attention and energy is devoted to the crisis points in the organic societal body. You go to where lightning is striking, and to the source of the strike.

Convoluted and harmful notions of sameness of treatment actually create inequity. Optimal wellbeing requires the particular attention that each child, family, and community uniquely needs. Simplistic adherence to treating *all people the same*, and other homogenous approaches prevent the honoring of true needs. It leads to a paving over of potholes in the name of not giving *special treatment* to any one sector of the road.

Oppressors have favorite sayings. One is, *You people don't take care of your own, so we have to do it.* Another bellows, *No one should focus exclusively on helping those people. That's not inclusive, patriotic, or peaceful. All people need help.* See the tactic inside their words.

Corrective treatment of crisis areas cures disparity and creates authentic equity free of supremacy culture. This is fundamentally different from preferential treatment that aims to create advantage and inequity. You cannot treat the consequences of oppression and human devaluation by not treating those consequences at all out of fear that it would be *preferential*. Watch for people who practice preference treatment that upholds supremacy while assailing targeted treatment that heals oppression. They are leading everyone off a high, steep cliff.

In a hospital emergency ward, nurses and doctors do not respond to patients according to an attitude and policy of artificial sameness. Patients would die. Instead, they turn their attention and resources toward those patients exhibiting the most critical need. This is the way of freedom work.

In epidemic situations, public health authorities do not ignore the influx of afflicted people emerging from similar geographies so that they can be proud that they *serve all people*. They trace the patterns of geographical origin and examine the unique factors within those populations that might be at the root of the epidemic. They understand that in an epidemic, the harmful contagion will eventually spread to other populations, to the entire society or humanity, if particular attention and treatment are not directed toward the immediately vulnerable. These authorities realize that as dysfunction and despair spread their awful wings, systemic resources and capacity will be depleted, jeopardizing all populations. They realize that the contagions that create crisis in a community often do not originate in that community but rather in the larger, colonizing ecology encompassing that community. And that the community currently in crisis is so because it has been made most vulnerable by society's preexisting simmering illness. Its latent epidemic waiting to burst forth through the geysers of material poverty and generational dehumanization.

Equity is not a utopia arrived at by treading a self-serving road of sameness. You do not maim a lion and then call yourself creating equity in the lion pride through your mission of equal treatment. You treat that which you have maimed. Most of all, you treat that which caused you to maim.

Action is the truest evidence of priority. We take action on behalf of what we truly value. Under-served communities are so because they are undervalued. With value comes service and investment. Thus, the fundamental question of prejudice. We do more for *our own* because we deem them valuable enough to give them everything. How do we define who is our own such that we are motivated to address the ailments, latent and erupted, of our collective humanity? Aversion to freedom work carries the suspect stench of valuing less those who exist on the wrong side of inequity's tracks.

Look what they got that we didn't get mentalities spring from a socialized place of insecurity and despair that is a natural offspring of fragmenting reality into competing pieces, individuals, and groups. The spoiled child pitches a fit inside the growth-challenged adult. The child does not care about the world. The child just wants ice cream. This spoiled child spirit needs to be raised to a relational maturity and sense of collective duty. Not raised by the adult who is being led by the spoiled child inside. Many favored people, carrying an immature, spoiled child spirit inside, do not want revolution. They resent it as giving ice cream to others and not to them. Even though they have been sick on an overabundance of ice cream all their lives.

MORALITY AND REVOLUTION

When, in a society, morality dies, all causes must be made personal. If not, not enough people will care. Moral arguments are crushed under the machinery of fear-based panic. Survival mode is not survival mode if it becomes chronic. Then, it is only destruction mode. In an immoral society, arguments against your people's oppression will not work. No one will care. Few will be living in high morality. Such a society depends on immorality for its social structure and paradigm of comfort and perceived security. Its people depend on immorality to sustain their generational way of life.

Morals may guide your revolution. They do not make effective medicine for virus-sickened hearts. And if you let your moral messaging fall into propaganda not tested by real reckoning, you lose touch with the raw clay of your revolution. Artificial, materialistic morality work sweeps its net shallowly, while the medicine for our healing swims in the depths of souls.

Self-concern is not intrinsically harmful. It is a survival trait. One that may be used as an instrument in the long journey toward collective human dignity. We alter the parameters of self-concern by creating new boundaries in our definition of *Us* and *Them*. When the *Us* comes to include the *Them*, we become newly motivated and activated to heal the web of life.

Humans are subjective in our taste in revolutions. The cause has to be convenient for us before we will consider it. It has to be relevant to us before we will taste it. It must be saving our own home from burning before we will jump up and join it. To work with this human condition, reflect often on how your revolution must feel to those who may be revolted by it. They will be good indicators of how your revolution may taste to more neutral people. What you are creating is a camp where all who are lost smell what is cooking over the fire and at least dare to approach.

YOUR REVOLUTION IS SACRED AND HOLY

Only a conquered soul and conditioned mind ask whether spirituality belongs in a revolution. Spirit, which is Love, is the only force that belongs in a revolution. Spirituality is freedom's fuel. Freedom's starlight. Freedom's oxygen, garden, and faithful flowing spring.

The first thing they will seek to take from you is your spirituality. Your way of keeping your soul alive and free. Your tether to your ancestors. The first slavery is a conquest of the soul.

We perceive sacredness and holiness as rare aberrations in the quilt of life. This is like seeing stars in the night sky as the only divine element in that high, black blanket, and missing that the entire sky is a miracle. Sacredness is everywhere. All things are holy. When we say, *That is a holy person*, we reveal our blindness to the holiness in each person. Holiness is a latent potential in souls. Freedom work touches this potential into life.

Spirituality is that way of living by which you forever birth the soul of the world out through the world of your soul. Spirituality is womb work. Mind your ways of faith. They will be your way back home.

If an intellect-focused force comes at you saying, *Leave behind your spirit, your soul, your heart*, then you gather your people, for you are surely being recruited for the cage.

177

All humans are orphans in this world, our souls separated from the womb that is the spirit world. This creates in us an inherent insecurity throughout life, a needfulness we try to fill many ways. Some fruitful, some ill-fated. This existential insecurity is only filled by our personal work to open our soul back to its origin. *Homecoming.*

Do you believe your people can be free? If the deepest part of you does not believe this, you will sabotage the journey to freedom. You will be your master's greatest champion. Inner belief work is the true work of revolution. A labor of faith in the sanctuary of the soul.

The life of your soul determines the soul of your life. Feed your soul and you feed your life. All lives have a soul. Some are well fed and vibrant. Others are starving and weakened. The soul of your life is a living thing. Care for it the way you care for your living things. How? By nourishing the life inside your soul.

Open the eyes of your soul and look at everything.
Know you are looking at Holiness. Act accordingly.

Two songs live in your soul. A sorrow song and a glory song. Sing the one that blesses your life with life. You are not a helpless leaf floating down an uncaring river. You are a river, full of sacred song. Water yourself all the way back to *wonder-full.* Inspire the choir that is your ancestral soul.

Freedom from oppression requires developing the ability to see souls. Until you can see souls, all you see is supremacy and inferiority, grave illusions and tainted mist. Practice seeing souls by practicing seeing your own soul. If you look and see a person, you are not looking. If you look and see all the people in that person, now you are truly looking. Now you are a seer of souls. Such vision is a filter that keeps the spirit of your work clean, purified. For pollution will be daily.

In this world, everything eats everything. It is the way of living things. Sky eats water. Water eats sky. Earth eats them both. Plants eat animals. Animals eat plants. Microbes eat them both. People eat everything. Everything eats people. Earth cultures say, *Eating is not what matters. What matters is the spirit in how you eat. Honor the life you eat. Honor its spirit and sacrifice. Honor its suffering. Show honor by how you live, fed by the nutrition of what you eat.* Another way to say this is: *What matters is how you relate to living things.* Relate with honor, or relate to desecrate. You can always choose.

Learning the difference between spiritual servitude and being a slave means everything. When you serve a divine calling, the spirit of what calls you keeps you free, regardless of how your offering is received by people. When you serve the conditioned calling of unfree people, now you are in the condition of being a slave.

The soul has a quality like the sun. It burns to be released, to radiate outward, to paint life in the palette of life. The soul cannot be satiated with dimness, with submitting to survive. It is only at peace in full shine. It is an appetite of Grace.

If you can feel the holiness of a moment,
you can be a womb for beautiful things.

When we speak of freedom, we do not mean whims or selfishness. We mean absolute annihilation of whatever is not the soul.

A monk sat by a river and pondered the desert. Then he walked up a mountain and pondered the valley. That night while sleeping, his soul gathered peace seeds. When he woke, he planted a whole new forest for the world. In your revolution, ponder Creation, life, often. Dream as though you are collecting divine flowers of Truth. Plant liberation where you go.

Spirituality is not just an aspect of revolution. It is the very nature of revolution. It is the marrow of revolution. Its tears. Voice. Heartbeat. Compass. In your bowed, prayerful petition to your Creator, you are asking not only how to revolt. You are asking for the continued will and strength to revolt. In the monsoon washing your soul thereafter, you receive your Grace calling by the moment.

When oppressors, living their lives trapped in suppressing others, suppressing their own guilt, gather to worship the Sacred, you can hear a pin drop in those worships. A repression sound. A quiet of conflict and contradiction soaked in inescapable guilt. A silence that sounds like suffering.

All striving for freedom is a prayer. A petition. An inward, outward, upward exclamation and rejoicing of the soul. It is vital that you gather peace inside your soul. Peace is your centerpiece as you work for freedom. Center peace.

No more words. No thoughts or actions. Just rebirth in the womb of silence. If your revolution will succeed, it will be because it found its stride in silence. Silence is a sacred womb. This world is in dire need of birthing. Open your being to the sweet Wordlessness that can infuse and renew your labor.

Spirituality is reborn through stillness. The noise of *civilized* worlds is designed to drown out true voice, distance people from their intuition, and separate them from each other. *Uncivilized.*

Spirituality is most fruitful when it is authentic soul soaking, not a periodic, obligated ritual to appease guilt and affirm goodness. True spirituality is a recognition of the oneness of life that clarifies a people's boundaries, integrity, and communal duty in the sacred web of life. It is not a battleground for differences among spiritual ways.

When the mind becomes detached from the spirit, from soulfulness, it loses the medicine it has as a natural part of our whole being. It becomes restrictive, infertile, desolate. It becomes a reservation, when before it was a boundless, thriving, wild territory. In order to control and exploit you, to neuter your power, oppressors and their culture have to condition you to exist only in the isolated reservation of the mind. Break free. Live across your many splendid acres.

If your soul is your center, how can spirituality not be at the heart of your liberation work? Oppressors try to separate spirit from life, which is why oppressor societies grow lifeless. There is no life without spirit. If spirituality, the living ways of your spirit, creates communion between you and all things, how can you work for freedom in all ways if you exclude the ways of your spirit? Oppressed, conditioned minds question whether spirituality belongs in healing and freedom work. This never occurs to those who are healing and on freedom's path. One of the first things oppressors demand when they invade and terrorize is that you get rid of your spirituality. Reclaiming your spirituality is one of the first steps toward regaining your freedom.

LOVE AND WHAT IS NOT LOVE

The bravest revolutions begin in the heart.

There is no freedom without Love. Love is freedom's atmosphere. Hate can strive for freedom, but hate can only achieve imprisonment. Hate is a tumor. Love is the medicine that cures supremacy-inferiority virus. Love is the antidote. It dissolves all high places and low places. What Love touches becomes light stumbling without equilibrium into everything that is not light. The collisions birth more light. Love is not always a flower. Love can be hard. It promises no perfections or absence of anger. But if you are brave enough to dare it as you work for freedom, you will taste the spice of healing. And it will be good.

A small, quiet woman went to the ocean, which recognized her infinite soul water and leapt into her ocean.

You are not here to discover the world. You are the world discovering itself. Behold the ocean that is your soul. Drown there so you may be all the way alive. Dilate. Burst. Surrender. Open. This is the divine condition we call Love.

How much of your Love will revolution require? All of it. You will not get away with portioning or rationing your Love, saving it for certain souls and not others. If you want your freedom fire to consume the whole forest, you will need to feed it the only fuel it accepts: all your Love.

If in your revolution you are unsure which way to go, Love is always the way to go. Let that impossible illumination be your North Star.

Self-hatred is an overlooked aspect of a revolution. You are asking people to act in Love for their people, when not only do some of them not Love their people, they do not Love themselves. Revolution depends on creating climates and incentives for people to heal into a new way of seeing and feeling about themselves. So they can be ground for collective Love.

Your oppressor's existence depends on a measure of hating your kind. Hatred is the only justification for monstrous ways. This is how oppressors solve their haunting cognitive dissonance of being a good person who treats an entire people monstrously. Hatred absolves them. It is their convenient confessional without the confession.

What is the immune system against this virus? Loving care between you and yourself, between your people and themselves. Only this energy is strong enough to fortify a people against the hostile, dehumanizing energy of oppression.

Saying you Love yourself but putting down your culture and heritage is like saying you Love maple syrup while you chop down the maple tree. Be careful not to catch anything from those who seem to always be sharpening their ax.

Like sunlight through glass, Love is magnified by our journeys through difficulty. In this rough landscape of challenge, we can often see the true glory of our monumental wealth as it resounds, in Love.

Only through the heart may we touch the soul.
And this, forever, is why we are here.

People will say they Love you, and it can feel like bondage. Love wants nothing from you. When Love announces itself, your soul will feel free. Open to that divine sky. If it feels like a cage, it is not Love, though Love may be present. Love itself feels like a million windows and doors. All of them open. Love feels like the sky.

Others will judge you.
Love will not judge you.
Believe in Love's idea of you.

If you choose prejudicial hate, the object of your hate will never go away, and you will have chosen perpetual inner suffering. Choose unconditional Love and the object of your Love will never go away. You will be wed to bliss.

Your soul conducts your revolution, for it is your aspect that most remembers and recognizes freedom. Your mind organizes your work, though that organization is destined to be like papers in the wind, disarrayed by freedom's entropy. Things grow wild as they grow free. They do not submit to rationale, order, structure, and control, those qualities of oppression. Freedom's structure is Love, which has no structure at all.

The bravest thing you can ever do in this world is to strip naked and open blatantly into pure Love. This is where revolutionary courage shows its sacred force.

If you take Love out of your revolution, your revolutionaries will eat each other alive. Competition and ego cannot be the foundation of your revolution. Your people need a more nutritious food.

Freedom work requires sustainable motives. Anger can be a righteous and propulsive fuel that benefits your revolution at times. It will get you far in short bursts. Ultimately it will deplete you and take your health. If your motives are not deeply rooted, deeply vital and nourishing, or if they burn bright then burn away, your energy and wellness will burn out with them.

If you want freedom but refuse to expose your heart to labor in the majestic field we call Love, perhaps it is not freedom you want. But ease. Freedom and Love are not bride and groom. They are one single, delirious matrimony. Inhale freedom and you will exhale Love. Inhale Love and you will exhale freedom. We are not speaking of soft Love, of easy, puffy, adorable Love. We speak here and now of the unconditional asking that is Sacredness.

They will plunder you. All of you. Love yourself with all the Love in the world. That will be your protection. Wrap your arms around your people and Love yourselves to freedom.

There will be days when the crying child inside every person you encounter crashes down on you, an ugly wave. On those days, be the ocean. Stay in Love. Your Love is a compassionate ocean larger than any suffering. You don't have to drown in the world's pain. You can drown that pain in your ocean of Love. For if you are alive, you are a breath of infinity. A bountiful thing.

Revolution, even against the worst of things, can be joyful, for it grows in the Love we share for the best of things. Operating from anger and hate, you eventually burn up. Operating from Love and what you Love, you tap a sustaining source. If you are going to walk across the wide desert, anger will get you a short distance fast. Once that adrenaline has passed and you are exhausted, the desert has its way with you. Love's water may propel you less dramatically, but you will survive the desert.

Stay close to what sacredly Loves you.
Stay even closer to what you sacredly Love.

Freedom is fueled by Love. Anything else leads to exhaustion, unwellness, dissipation of energy and motivation, and eventually to the death of freedom, which is a living thing. Freedom is an atmosphere of Love. Not of resentment, bitterness, hatred. Love for yourself and your people. Love for Creation and Creator. Love for life.

A child brings her mother a handful of sand. Smiling, she says, *Mommy, I brought you some pearls I found on the beach!* Her little face is radiant with sunlight and Love. Her mother sees the sand in her child's hand, and also the Love and joy in her child's heart. Tears spill down her cheeks, catching sunlight. She says, *How kind of you, Sweetheart! These are the most beautiful pearls I have ever seen! What a wonderful gift.* They share a hug that warms them the rest of the day. This is how we keep each other well along the freedom way. To imagine together the pearls in hearts and see past the grinding dirt.

Your anger, though righteous, will never be medicine for those you hope to change. You cannot change them anyhow. But your Love is a tonic with no boundary. A sweet contagion for souls. Be Love's infectious agent. Permit yourself your full range of human emotions, for you are on a human journey. See, though, if you can channel all your feelings into a fertility, an ability to fill your soul with energy that heals you and gives you life. If your emotions are rivers, follow them to arrive at the ocean that is inner peace.

You can stop wandering the universe seeking a home. Love is your true planet. If you want to be truly free, sing your Love song everywhere. No conditions. Just the relentless outpouring of your pure, miraculous Love notes. Just how willing are you to be a Lover? Life forever challenges you with possible reasons not to Love. These are your prison doors. Will you enter? Or will you challenge yourself to remain free? Only one path births your liberation. Not the submissive idea of Love. The sacred bravado of Love. The mighty blasphemy against fear. The open field and endless sky of your existence. Love is your true planet. If it were not for Love, you would have nowhere to pour your soul waters. No basin, no riverbed, no waterfall. Were it not for Love, you would have no height from which to drop your tears. No tree, no cloud, no atmosphere. Were it not for Love, you would have no ground from which to rise. No earth, no garden, no valley. It if were not for Love, your glory would have no way of existing in this world. And this glorious world would have no way of existing in you. Hallelujah. For there is Love.

Hate is like an infant in a high chair terrified of the food being brought in a spoon toward its mouth. The infant sees the food coming. Its arrival feels inevitable. This inevitability is what causes the infant to panic, rage, kick and scream, go blind with fear. The infant in this moment is so filled with inflammatory chemicals, it can no longer function with intelligence or self-preservation. Now the baby is lost in destructiveness. All that matters is avoiding what cannot be avoided. The food. The foreign thing that seems to have power. Real power. The baby is mad and willing to destroy itself, the food, the one who brings the food, everything. This is a portrait of hate and how it brings us to infancy in the face of change, in the face of freedom.

Hatred can change a person's molecular biology. This transformation can be passed on genetically, leaving the next generation more biologically vulnerable to hatred. Even to hatred for the same groups as the generation before. Hate, mild aversion, dislike, and fear can all be coded into the soul's preferences and aversions.

Your revolution does not have to be angry, ugly, or hurtful. It can be the most Loving, caring, and nurturing space in the world. It can be a safe space, an oasis your people come to for respite. To feel supported, understood, and affirmed. A place where they can feel for the first time in their lives they are beautiful and they belong. This takes deep devotion to your personal and collective wellness, and to the spaces you create together. It takes a soul decision that says, *Love got us here across the ages and generations. Love will take us home.*

Actual Love is not a flowery emotion. It is a divine looking glass allowing you to see through ugliness and imperfection, all the way into the soul. Love gives you eyes for seeing sacred beauty. For revealing the ethereal world in the mundane world. Love lifts the somber veil of your blindness. Love says, *Behold, I have given you a life of* miracles. *See the face of this Glory. Do not stand guard against it. Let down your walls. Dare nakedness. I will bless your courage with a life of unreasonable Grace.*

A soul walked into a vase shop looking for a vase to take home and place by the bed. The shop owner showed the soul around, pointing out an endless array of beautiful vases gleaming in drapes of sunlight. Over and over, the shop owner said to the soul, *Why don't you take that one? It was crafted by a legendary artist from minerals gathered from a sacred river. Why don't you take that one? It was made by a monk on a mystic mountaintop. Why don't you take that one? It holds the highest price, the most elite renown.* The soul listened politely. Something caught the soul's eye. A vase poor of conventional beauty was sitting in dust on the floor, unwarmed by any sun in the room. The vase was cracked along its belly. Its shape spilled out into irregularity. Its lips were a jagged mess. Its base a lopsided misfortune. And its color was a confusion of hues, splashes of apologies. The soul picked up the vase and smiled, saying, *I will take this one.* The shop owner frowned. *But why, when you could have such beauty and perfection, would you choose a haggard jumble of defect and shame? That vase has been dropped and broken countless times. It has been sitting there on the floor for years. No one wants it.* The soul answered contently, *What other vessel in this place would more deeply appreciate my Love?*

Friend, if you have been paying attention to this story, you see that each of us is an ugly vessel, divinely beautiful in the eyes of Sacred Love.

Love is the sun freedom orbits.
If you don't orbit Love, you don't have freedom.

Remember when you were a child and in certain magical moments your heart felt so much joy and Love, it felt like

189

you were about to burst? You still have the same heart. Bring back the burst. The heart of joy and Love is not a physical organ. It is a channel within your soul. An eternal river. It cannot be transplanted out of you. What you felt once, you can feel again. Even if it has been far too long. If we are going to be free of oppression, we must grant ourselves joy, a jewelry around the sun that is Love. No matter what you have gone through or are going through, you can feel that bursting joy and Love again. Like all things, it takes practice. The act of nurturing a thing into habit. Joy and Love are habits. Vital instruments in the revolution toward a world that is free for all souls. If you are going to do your daily labor, make sure you feed yourself your daily bread. Joy and Love are among those. Eat plenty. *All our relations.*

No revolution whose deepest objective is the body or spirit death of others is a true revolution. The sun of social healing only turns toward life. We become so intertwined with, so attached to and diluted by our rancor and resentments, the idea of Loving others is painful for us. We react against it as though we are being asked to boil our own skin. If you reach this place of bruised condition, have hope and take note. The end of your suffering is always within you. You may have developed an appetite for bitterness and aversion. But your heart forever has a sweet tooth for Love's confection. Feed it the sugar it craves.

Your anger will not save you. Only Love can do that.

Do you understand that you cannot live forever in your anger? Justified or not, your anger is an acid. It does damage to your entire being. It scalds those you Love. It burns to ash the very dream you dream. Cultivate your anger. Shape it into a force that moves you into change. Change in you. Change beyond you. Be an alchemist pouring Grace on a justified fire and making it salvation rain.

Do you have a right to your oppression wounds and anger? A more meaningful question is, *Do you have a duty in how you use that woundedness and anger?* You can use your wounds as instruments in the ancestral surgery to excise the pus of supremacy and oppression. The choice is yours. Do you perform healing, or do you perform harm?

Why is Love in the world? To teach us freedom. Why are we born? To journey freedom. Why do we die? To reunion with freedom. This life is not about control and conquering. It is for the brave breath of being free. Some dances we do on earth grow sour on the vine of eternity. Human quarrel always feels justified to the quarreler. But to the rest of Creation witnessing, we are fooling ourselves into oblivion. The song of life is a single note. Love.

What would you do to make a butterfly feel safe in your palm? Love the whole world like that. Especially you. Make delicate things feel safe with you. After all, you too are a delicate thing. May you find the gentle holiness in your night, your day, your life, and through it, be born anew. Living sacredly, you too can make all things new.

LIGHT THE FIRE OF YOUR REVOLUTION

Revolution does not always move like wildfire. Sometimes it is a slow moss, blooming on trees. Patience and endurance are sacred tactics. In time, they overtake the forest, bring softness back into the world.

You do not have to start your revolution fire by running around the forest dramatically burning down every tree. You can start small and intimate, gathering kindling with your close circles of relation, joining in gentle breathing on the first sparks. As the flame is born and grows more assured of itself, you can work outward into the larger circles of relation. A small warming fire in the cold and dark can become a sunrise that seduces the world.

Know when to teach. And when to listen.

You do not lead a revolution. A revolution leads you. When the fire in you matches the fire in the world, synchronicity does its sacred work. Stay in the humility of your soul. The public show will try to seduce you. Stay faithful to your calling. Serve the greater yearning.

Don't ask others to illuminate you. If you want to be light, take the candle that is your soul and light your own being. Practice inspiring yourself to freedom.

Some will call you a prophet. Do not get drunk on that seductive wine. When a squirrel prepares for winter, it is a prophet. A tree dropping its leaves is a prophet. A chick in a high nest, nervous before its first flight, a prophet. Lovers, opening their tender hearts for what's to come, paired prophets. Do not say who is or is not a prophet. Prophets are everywhere.

Revolution is not a conformity parade. Disagreement is intrinsic to the cause. Stay close together around the fire of your collective Love for each other. Hold that root. Let your disagreements move through you, not undo you.

While you are here, you might as well say the truth you were sent here to say. We are all just messengers. And the message is always holy. Open up. Gather your sacred water. Pour.

When it really hurts, have hope.
You are in the birth canal.

A new world is a big thing to have come through a birth canal. We will suffer to deliver this baby. If only we could recognize the moment of our deliverance. It is here. When your days are hard, deep breath now, dear soul. Your sun is already rising. It will be divine.

Revive your languages. Restore your customs. Recover your land. Heal your relations. Host peace. Give ear to your ancestors. Weave new stories. *Rethrone* your native beauty. Distill medicine from your suffering. Build a fire. Welcome those who Love your flames. Ceremony the night. Make dream offerings. Soul-bless the day.

Learn the song that free things sing.
From the throttling throat to the beating of wings.

If you plant your freedom garden in unfertile soil, the seeds will not sprout, the blooms will not blush, the pollinators will not arrive. You need the rich black soil that has grown unimpressed with comfort and desire. You need the soil of souls who look in the mirror of their lives and see nothing but a worthiness only Sacredness can decide.

Go around the world with your soul and destroy all the empires. Those on land, in the mind, and in the spirit of things.

May we honor the sacred web of life. It is our only way forward. May we be on earth with each other in a good way. May we care about the freedom of others as much as we care about our own freedom. May we bring Sacredness back into human life. That we may touch our suffering and transform it into a knowing kind of peace.

Many are comfortable with ideas of freedom. They curate theories of freedom. Enjoy freedom discussions. Blanket themselves in freedom symbols. But when true freedom with all its unconditional conditions approaches them, these same purveyors of freedom run for their lives. Truly, they run for their deaths. They don't want the fire that would burn them back to life.

Humans are herd animals. Power and harm live in this truth. We can both influence ourselves into slavery and out of slavery. *Exodus.*

Your soul does not yearn for you to bring it things from the world. It yearns for you to bring it out into the world. Show your soul. That is how you change the world. You can feed your soul the world. Just make sure you feed the world your soul.

Have wild feelings. Do not tame them. Give up your old life of slavery and fear. Something both divine and practical can live inside freedom. It is possible to be responsible and still change the world.

You are not the brittle thing you imagine.
You are spirit, a breathing prayer. Imagine that.

For the rest of your life, labor beside only revolutionaries, activists, peace doulas, and freedom dancers. It is time to rebirth the world.

If you are too consumed with planning your revolution, you may never act to revolt. Planning eats up time. Time passage insulates oppressive conditions from assault. Too much structure chokes the life out of your revolution. At some point your freedom work must freestyle, must become music, rhythmic, intuitive, unpredictable. Flow and spark with euphoria and divining. If your freedom notes are known and anticipated, they can be drowned out, averted, easily countered. And if you are following a script, how can you be following your soul?

Oppression is contemporary, trendy, fashionable.
Keep your eyes open and your freedom fire fresh.

If you bring your freedom fire to people expecting them to gratefully accept it, you will be disappointed. Many people, contradicting their own souls, do not want freedom. Build your freedom fire where you are. Stay with it. Be at peace with it. Who wants freedom will arrive, drawn by light and warmth. No matter their fears.

If your revolution is not ancestral, descendant, and personal, it is not a revolution. If it is not of family and the people, it is not a revolution. If it is not societal and global, it is not a revolution. A deep enough ripple touches and is touched by all the water. All the shore.

As the sun goes down, some grieve sunlight. Some grow anxious of the dark. Others give thanks for daylight received and the night of restoration ahead. You can use these hopeful, grateful souls as candles when the revolution light flickers and dims.

Go searching for anything that acts like freedom. When you find it, do not lose yourself in it. If you become its follower, you will lose your freedom. Become its friend.

Some want the world and themselves to change so badly, they cry, *Action!* They are offering themselves as kindling for revolution fire. Accept their offering. Some will die before letting you move them from their inertia. No need to push against boulders when you can pick up willing stones and sail them in the wind.

People Love sunrise and sunset but write no poems to the sun that lives in between. Celebrate the modest marrow of freedom progress that becomes the acclaimed freedom bones. Celebration can be the flame of your intermediate sun.

When supremacy is dying, it does not go with ease or grace. It soils itself. In this dying season, it is on us to decide our world. Do we endure the death wail of supremacy and its violent, panicked clinging to the world, and let it die? Or do we succumb to our acute discomfort and let supremacy be?

We are in that time when the river reckons with itself. Two currents gain increasing form and pull. One stream leads us deeper into the ominous mangroves of suffering. The other stream courses evermore into life. We are here now. We cannot make this day go away. It is time to choose.

You are not weaving an entirely new thing. Take power from this. You are mending an ancient thing that has long endured. Your potential in this is as strong and promising as is the sacredness you mend. You are not inventing freedom. Do not burden yourself so. You are bringing light to an unjust eclipse. You are sparking an ember that wants to be renewed. Your path is not impossible. Or even improbable. If you blow on a living ember, you will have your fire. Freedom is not a pipe dream. If you do freedom work, freedom is promised.

HEAL YOUR REVOLUTIONARY SOUL

Oh, how powerful your soul is.
If only you believed you are a soul.

So much of our struggle is because we believe we are nothing more than our vulnerable, needful, temporal body. A soulless culture conditions us to disbelieve in our true essence and nature. You are a soul, indivisible, irreducible, inconceivable, agape with life. This is your true size. Your true power. Your true calling.

Your soul is the sun inside you. Stay in your light.

When it feels as though the sun is crumbling, and your panic is a rising sea, return to your breathing. It is a messenger whispering: *I was made for this. Even now, I am bliss.* You were made for this. Stay with your breathing. It is your medicine, home, peace sky, freedom.

Don't let those who consider themselves enlightened dim your actual light. You have access to the same sun they do. A sun that also goes by the name of Truth.

Gratitude dissolves many sorrows. Life is not an entitlement. Life is a holy miracle. Freedom for your soul begins with comprehending the soul of freedom: *Grace.*

Pain is a soil where the seeds of peace can grow.
If you have pain, you have a starter kit for peace.

You don't have to beat yourself up to grow. You need no whipping. The pain you are in is motive enough to change. When the pain comes, let it do its mystic work. Don't chase it away. Don't hoard it. Breathe. It wants to break open your inner prisons. Give it absolute, top-level, classified permission.

The first time she enforced her boundary and refused to let herself be violated, dishonored, harmed, she was terrified. Her terror was the birth water of her freedom.

Your boundary need not be an angry electric fence that shocks those who touch it. It can be a consistent light around you that announces: *I will be treated sacredly.* Exude your mantra, you precious soul where peace resides: *I will be treated sacredly.* This is how you reclaim your sovereignty. In the light that goes before you.

If you find yourself no longer tolerant of people harming or dishonoring you, toast yourself. You are healing. Boundaries are a sign you are claiming your sacred sovereignty. And, therefore, the beautiful possibilities of your life. Only you can determine how people treat you, which is nearly the same thing as how you treat yourself. Here's to your freedom.

You aren't here to cure other people's illness. Try, and they will suck your energy all the way to death. You will lose yourself. Your relations will lose you. You are here as medicine for your own healing, which becomes medicine for your relations. Still, they must take the medicine available to them. Do not obligate yourself to feed a resistant adult in baby-state. Nurture your own medicinal life. Have faith its produce will be shared in the circle where souls are ready.

Grow willing and able to endure social retribution and ridicule. Revolution muscles include common purpose, spiritual calling and faith, hope and endurance, inner stillness, patience, joy, humility, and holy courage. Exercise these muscles daily.

Kindness is a kind of sun for the soul.
Open to it. Grant it. Live in it.

Kindness is a lubricant for freedom work. Especially when challenged by what the work unearths. Your tendency may be to burrow down into unkindness. This defense mechanism smothers your wellness, takes away all the air. Freedom is a breath work. Stay in the breeze that is kindness. May your Loving kindness travel far, find fertile earth, and become good seed.

Kindness is a mental health practice. A freedom device. When you are kind to yourself or others, you create a healing cascade of chemicals and spirit in your brain, body, and being. In your behavior, experiences, and reactions. Unkindness creates the opposite effect. If you want to heal, kindness is the path. If you want to be free, kindness is the key. If you want wellness, treat yourself and others in the ways of wellness, which are woven in strands of kindness. Mental health isn't an accident or an endowment. It is a creative practice within your holistic health. Here's to your lifelong art.

You have lived long enough. Suffered and endured long enough. Loved long enough. Witnessed and grieved long enough. You are qualified. For what? Everything. Take your freedom, dear soul. Like a ripe fruit from a summer tree, pluck your providence. Let this be the season you grant your soul permission to sing.

As you grow deep peace in your soul, predatory things will appear on rooftops and power lines, coming for crumbs of your peace. Peaceful things will appear on branches and blossoms, coming to share with you, peace for peace. Things will be drawn to you. Just don't be drawn away from your peace.

Your history is not your master. You are not its slave.
Your next moment is always a freedom door.

You are not obligated to suffer.
You are not obligated to suffer.

You are not obligated to suffer.

This day is a new land. Breathe and greet it gratefully. Bring water. Leave some habits behind. Take new trails. Look around. You will see, feel, be moved by things you have not before. Learn to be new. You will know wonder again.

This change you are considering. That terrifies you with what could go wrong. Have you considered what could go wrong if you don't change? What already is wrong because you have not changed? Have you weighed the worth of what could go right? Remember, your whole life has been change. You're still here.

After fleeing yourself, being with yourself can become a kind of bliss. Welcome home. After a lifetime of running from yourself, it can be scary to learn to thrive in solitude and inner living. One day, though, you will wonder how you ever lived without the companionship of your own soul. The one who wants you most will always be you. As you heal and grow, you discover that your painful longing wasn't for others. It was for the sublime part of you that you had not yet known or lived in. Once you arrive there, all other relationships feel less like an anxious need and more like a light and joyful gift. You stop grasping and start savoring. Like when you dance in moonlight without trying to bottle the moon.

May your wondrous heart and spirit imitate sky today. Wide-open, unencumbered, and light as air. May the womb of life wrap its sacred self around you, a ceremonial blanket of care and assurance. May you be birthed into the bright light of your purpose and calling. May your giftedness spill out into the world, a treasure for all living things. May you suckle from the milk of true, everlasting peace, and sing a song that speaks your splendid soul.

When your heart is so tender you feel your light touch would burst it like a water drop, this is your moment. Rejoice. For you are at the birth of healing. When it hurts, it is time. With Love, follow your ache. It will guide you, a faithful friend, into the light. When it hurts, grow softer. Turn your earth. So you can be soil for the seeds of healing. When it hurts, grow softer. So the pain can get out. So Love's medicine can get in.

You've been through some things.
That's why your spirit sings.

Pain is a mystic kindness that tunes our soul instrument to the music of Grace. When we use our struggle in a self-Loving manner, life has a way of purifying us, revealing what is real, clearing our vision, and grounding us in purpose. Suffering is a filter that cleanses our soul, lifting our sacred song from the sediment into the sky of our revival. You've been through some things. This, dear soul, is why your spirit sings. It knows Grace. And is forever grateful.

It hurts when you drift away from your soul.
Come back home.

Reframe your shame. Shame is a social disease. A social infection. But also a window. A door. People project ideas on to you from shared prejudices about people like you. The kindred sicknesses of supremacy and inferiority find their way to you through social shaming. Generational oppression is transmitted into you through shame's needle. When you feel guilt or shame about who you are, this is an opportunity to practice Love for yourself, and for growth and healing. When you feel shame, look through that window and examine its roots. This demystifies your spiritual chains. Then, apply the medicine of whatever ceremony brings you back to Loving yourself and those who are shamed like you. Feelings of shame are a doorway to your personal and collective freedom. Move through the shaded tenderness out into the brightness of your beautiful life. And the beautiful lives of those like you.

This work you are doing to heal your life. It is a mountain stream. Soon, you reach the ocean. Even the faintest, slowest trickle is on its way to the wide-open sea of freedom. Be gentle. Float the current.

When you enter a sacred sanctuary, instantly you grow quiet, still, in awe. You leave your chaos outside and humble yourself to the air of Sacredness. Maybe you bow or kneel or pray. Your heart opens. Your thoughts grow softer. You show respect to this holy space by not using foul language or behavior. You don't pollute or trash this space. You believe this sanctuary is sacred. So you treat it as such. Now, dear soul... imagine if you believed you yourself were a sacred sanctuary. How then would you treat yourself? Because you are. Sacred. Sanctuary. *Hush now*. Behold your holiness. Proceed.

Face the rules of your childhood. This is an early step toward freedom. Face all the rules. Undress them. Examine them nude of authority, in daylight. All the rules now living in you like sludge: Emotion. Religion. Behavior. Speaking. Silence. Questioning. Following. Leading. Family. Friendship. Loving. Hating. Body. Learning. Memory. Romance. Ending. Beginning. Dying. Living. Working. Earning. Spending. Believing. Choosing. Face all the rules. Line them up naked and shivering. Appraise them. Decide. Discern which rules to release. Which to burn. Which to carry forward lightly.

203

Release even your rules about rules. Follow your spirit. Let that be your Golden Rule.

They will call you angry, hostile, a threat. When this happens, shape shift. Become a lion standing between your cubs and predators. No need to posture or roar. Your strength is in the ferocity of your Love for your people, for your kind, for all kinds. This energy announces itself through your steadfast presence. Your aura of determination. Become a lion. Stand in place. Do the work.

Before they try to destroy you, they must convince their kind that you are not human. This gives them permission for murder. Often it is the only way they allay their guilt: not reckoning with their pathology and harm. But by reducing you. Do not shrink or narrow. Stay supple and in blush. Live in your full humanness. Do not help their cause.

When you feel stuck and don't know which way to go with your freedom work, let your *Self* die. Lose all your ideas, especially your beliefs. Humble yourself to Spirit and the cacophony of your ancestors. Stop creating and let yourself be created. Start over in emptiness and nakedness.

Your revolution needs continuous purification. It requires that you spend time in the desert. In a desert's drastic environment, impurities are drawn out from the soul, heart, mind, and body. Desert is another form of water even in its aridity. Absence of water makes desert life ache for water, obsessed with water, ready for water. Desert is a yearning flow of water spirit. Revolution attracts corruption and pride pollution into revolutionaries. Lance out these energies by bathing in what forms of desert feel helpful. Let your soul leave you and be cleansed by nonhuman elements. It will return renewed for your cause. Purify personally and collectively. Gathering in a sacred way purifies. Ceremony will keep you strong.

She stopped waging war against herself and realized all her soul ever wanted was ease. Not battle. Breeze.

Maybe you have fought all your life. Fighting is all you know. But, splendid soul, only when you are capable of keeping peace inside your soul, can you be free. The world wants you oppressed. But oppression requires that you oppress yourself. That you be your own constant overseer. Your own whip and chains. Maybe your generations have passed down to you their inner harshness, their guilt, shame, criticism, punishment, exhaustion, and self-neglect. Now you believe that to be a good person, to make your people proud, you must batter yourself. Forever. This is not Love. It is a lie sowed by the original battery and harm. Precious soul, if you are here, alive and pulsing, you have a chance to be the one in your lineage to put down the lash and pick up the light of freedom. You can do the personal and collective Love work to begin to believe in the goodness, the power, the promise of ease. No more dis-ease. No more battle. Just breeze.

Imagine a fire you keep in the wilderness. It is cold and dark, so everyone wants to come near the fire to be warmed and have their lives illuminated. Out of Love and compassion, you want them to be fed that, too. But if you keep focusing on gathering more people to the fire and keeping them at the fire as long as they need or want, eventually the fire will die. You are the only one able to keep this fire, for it is your soul fire. Consistently tend your fire so it may remain a source of warmth, light, comfort, and safety. A fire needs fuel and air. You are the one to provide those things in an essential way. Other fires are communal. People may join in tending those communal fires. Your soul fire fundamentally depends on you, even if others can provide offerings. Your fire is your personal duty.

If you want to truly be free,
you must stop oppressing your own soul.

Have hope. All your life, people have taught you to oppress your own soul. Good news: For the rest of your life, you are going to learn freedom. You are going to learn in swirls and circles, not in straight lines. Cultivate patience with this journey. Yes, you are learning freedom. No more fear-soaked negative inner talk. Practice positive, affirmative, liberation talk and behavior for 10 seconds. Sustain it for 30 seconds. Keep building your freedom muscles. One day, a sunrise you have never felt before. One that warms your bones. A promissory note that says, *This sun lives inside you, and is eternal.* On that day, when your soul power overcomes your fears and false ideas, you, dear one, will taste freedom. Once you taste freedom, you will lose your taste for anything that is not freedom. And your living will feel like a gift of unremitting Grace. Souls will drink from your fountain, become fountains, nurture suckling fountains, and this tender world will run wild in a new way that is whole and good.

Would you like to hear an epic Love story?
You. Healing. From all of it. And living free.

Write your own legendary Love story. Live in it. Your freedom from woundedness is not a fantasy. Someone else healing you? Now that is a fantasy. Healing is in your genetics. You are programmed to take the damage and turn it into divine beauty. Healing was your first language. You can always regain your native tongue. May you be free, you sweet soul. May you be free.

Your wellness is the greatest threat to those who would oppress you. Your legacy and revolution are a matter of how healthful you can be with other humans, with the world, and with yourself. BeLoved, your career accomplishments are a thin streak of light compared to the sun dance of your soul accomplishments. Garden your mind, heart, body, spirit, and relations. Garden them daily with joy and gratitude. Give up worrying about pleasing, accolades, and applause. Hold a gathering of two around a mud puddle. Share a sermon with the trees. Write a poem and publish it in a child's heart. Laugh deeper than you fret. Cry like your tears are precious gifts to be shared. Break bread. Break soul. Break order. Jump into the sacred water of Loving you for being you: the first step in cleansing from social poisoning and offering your purified self to the world. Humanity is bursting into its new era of ancestral ways. Be the light in that luminous sky. Greed and plunder are obsolete. Communion is the paradigm about to reign. It starts with you gathering your pieces. Be good to you. Be good to you. Be good to you.

You will never feel ready for the blessings that scare you most. Readiness has nothing to do with it. If it makes no sense to you at all, it might be because blessings could not care less about your sense of things. They just want to show you the impossible is possible. Blessings aren't about you and your logic or reason. Blessings use you for a much greater purpose. If you jump into your blessings, you may find your blessings have already jumped into you. Don't worry about whether you are ready. Your blessings have been readied for you. You aren't the baker of the blessings. You are the bread your blessings are here to bake. Now jump into the fire that is your purpose. If it makes no sense, that's because your purpose laughs at your nonsense. And goes on baking your sweet life.

Always look for new ways to Love yourself.

You have not yet arrived at the final frontier of Loving yourself. More land awaits. And remember, your Loving of you is not for you. It is for the world. Each of us has been given life so we may make an offering of our life. Do not follow the hyper individualistic ways of an unwell culture. Hoarding for yourself is not Loving yourself. Nurturing yourself so you may pour fresh water for others, this is Love. Be generous in nurturing yourself. Take all the moments. Look under all the stones. Permit yourself euphoria and ease. Brew your tears into serenity stew. Let your leaves go with the wind. Embroider peace across your tender heart. Pick your joy flowers randomly. Acquaint your tongue with morning dew.

Forgive yourself and grow.
Forgive yourself and grow.
Forgive yourself and grow.

Forgiving yourself is how not to drown in guilt and shame. How to stay on the shore of freedom. If you can forgive yourself, you loosen one of the main knots of oppression. Guilt is our cage, warden, and judicial conviction. You are worthy of feeling good about yourself today. Unconditionally. When you feel good about yourself, you make offerings to the world filled with goodness. Be a good nest. Forgive yourself, reckon, heal, grow, and glow. Watch the beauty born that takes wing and blesses the sky of all relations with paradise.

What the full moon does to the night sky,
let your own Love do to your precious heart.

Dear heavenly one. If only you could see your true brilliance with your first eyes, before you gathered false ideas of you.

Look again, washed clean. All the light you crave lives inside you. Soul light is always in you. Illuminate yourself. Sleep in awe under that starry sky.

She planted three seeds over and over
that changed her life:
I. Am. Enough.

It's your soil (soul). Nobody else's.
Plant good seeds.

A thoughtful wind, sent by Grace, moves across your face. It asks of you a favor. *Remember peace.* Your true home.

Peace is a consequence.
Be the cause.

If it feels like it is healing your soul, open to it, even if you cannot yet understand it. Flowers don't ponder the sun. Some pondering traps us in quicksand. Some pondering helps set us free. Trust your soul.

Do not wait for the right condition to be at peace.
You are alive. That is the right condition.

You deserve Love, peace, kindness in your life. Never deny yourself these foods for the soul. If you feel undeserving of the essence of life, it is time, dear soul, to feed your essence with life. Massage your tender heart until it opens like a flower. And in those early moments when it dares to expose its sacred yearning, let inside what is beautiful in this world to heal what hurts you. Your life does not have to be what it has been. Goodness knows, you are worthy of goodness. It is waiting for you, even as you struggle to believe. Taste what is possible. Grow your appetite for Love, peace, and kindness. Learn to crave and cradle these gifts. If they show up in your life, do not question the timing or logic. Part open your heart and bravely take in the awesome grace of unreasonable glory. Let yourself be blessed.

Deep breath, dear one.
Good things are already growing.

She woke one day believing in her healing more than she believed in her suffering. Her soul rejoiced and flowered. Belief is how you water your soul garden. Belief doesn't grow from a beautiful life. A beautiful life grows from belief.

The one who cares enough to remove the splinter will
always be blamed for the pain. Be a healer anyway.

Remember when you were a child and you had a splinter? You were in pain and scared that something foreign and hurtful was in you. A certain helpless fear crept over. Maybe your parent was the compassionate one with the strength and skill to help you remove the splinter. But you were scared. As your parent took your hand, your fear grew. You panicked, sensing that the splinter coming out was going to hurt even worse for a moment. You didn't want to cross that threshold even as you were desperate for relief. As your parent began to work the tweezers against your skin, your tenderness screamed. You screamed. In your mind, your parent was hurting you. You may have even said hurtful things to your parent. You begged them to stop. To wait. Your parent knew the splinter needed to come out now or it would only become more deeply embedded. Your parent was following Love's urgency to help relieve your pain even as the remedy was so painful. When the splinter was finally removed, tears of relief gushed down your little face.

Something else gushed, too. Gratitude for your parent, that they Loved you enough to take your hand and help remove the source of your pain. This, dear one, is what it means to give yourself to the healing of souls. You are touching the most tender places in others. They may see you as the source of the pain. The divisive presence disrupting their fraudulent peace. Remain rooted in your truth: that you are so on fire with a Love-soaked sacred calling to respond to the urgency of Spirit and ancestors, that you will give yourself to treating the source of our collective pain. Make no mistake. We are in great pain. Many do not recognize the source pathologies of oppression, supremacy, and dehumanization. Many do not even realize they are suffering, that they are passing on the viral contagion. But you can be assured, as you touch the generational splinter, a great cry will come forth. Some will be well enough to be grateful for your offering. Some will see you as the source of the pain. Be faithful. Touch the tender wound. Grasp the splinter. Despite all resistance, do the collective healing work. You were given life for this. You are the sublime, sufficient instrument of an unconditional, ever amazing Grace.

Oh, dear one. You have been misled.
Your tenderness won't hurt you. It will save you.
Let. Your. Heavenly. Tears. Flow.

Don't be afraid to treat yourself sacredly. If you haven't always treated yourself so well, it can feel strange, uncomfortable, even vulnerable to treat yourself sacredly. As though you don't deserve it. As though it won't and shouldn't last. Especially if the people in your life don't treat themselves sacredly, or didn't treat you sacredly while you were growing up. Breathe peace now, dear one. Even small, bashful steps will get you to a sacred life. Sacredness is a habit. In a world that pollutes, cheapens, and desecrates the sacred, it is up to you to champion, celebrate, and role model living sacredly. Don't be afraid to believe you are a sacred thing. Don't be afraid to call yourself sacred. See what miracles happen when a sacred thing exists as a sacred thing. You have so many soulrises left in your life. And you are ever worthy of beautiful things. What are your sacred ways? Naming them brings them to life.

Your feelings don't arrive to harm you.
They arrive to lead you back to you.
Follow them.

Reflect on your journey. Find the treasure in it. Appraise your soul as worthy. Live as such. By far the greatest impediment to a beautiful life is our own belief that we are not worthy of a beautiful life. May you sing a new song in your soul that drenches your bones and marrow with permission to heal, grow, shine, swoon, surrender, release, joy make, peace plunder, open wide, Love big, dive deep, leap high, free fall through fate until you land in a living dream you wanted but never thought possible. Just maybe, your life ahead is not wed to your life that's been. Just maybe something beautiful is coming. Maybe it is already here. Drop a tear. Pour that blessing water over your fear. What you see as a wall is an open window. All things are possible if you believe. Reappraise everything. You haven't seen anything yet. To your eyes, it may be wearing a disguise. But be assured. Beautiful is already here.

Beautiful Soul.
Take off your heavy clothes of identity.
Have no idea who you are,
so who you are can be set free.

Paint a beautiful new world inside your mind. When the paint dries, create a gallery and invite everyone. The most glorious discovery of your life will always be learning you. You are the key to your own freedom. Discovering you will always be worth the labor. Journey beautifully.

Paradise is not a place.
It is a condition of the heart.

Bless your heart, Beautiful Soul. Bless your own heart. All the kindness you share with others, share with your heart. It has been on such a long journey. Sometimes it says to you, *Wait... Can we please rest here a while?* Give it what it needs. Grow quiet and listen. It will tell you. In response say, *Tonight I am staying in with you. No more running the streets looking for Love songs, when I can be with the source of sacred music. Tonight, my heart, I dance with you.*

But have you congratulated yourself for the progress no one knows about? Take that bow. Celebrate your progress along your freedom way. Celebration feeds you many things, including medicine in brain and body chemicals that soothe and heal your entire body and soul. Celebrate the grand gains and the smallest sand grains. Celebrate the private and the public things. All of it.

If you are wondering what you have
to offer the world,
it was always you.
Your singularity makes you priceless.

You are not here to imitate. You are here to illuminate. Only your unique light can do that. If every seashell on the beach were the same, you would not pause in wonder at any of them. Only by showing us how your soul sees this world can you offer us a new window into seeing this world. Do not fear having a unique perspective. Even if you are the only one who has ever lived and had your perspective. Especially then. You are not here to conform. Anyone can do that. You are here to be you. To express you. When you move through your fear of standing out, you become a divine window through which we look and see a shimmering new aspect of our collective truth. You will not be doomed by expressing your soul's clarity. You will be anointed by your own truth. The anointing will spread among kindred souls. Then among those who doubted your epiphany. You yearn to make an offering of your life. To add your kindling to our earthly fire. If you can heal, grow, and be willing to stand absolutely alone, you will find a tide of kindred souls who stand with you. Freedom doesn't gestate in the womb of conformity. It is birthed from the womb of your purposeful, singular truth. Be that rarest kind of light.

What if. Your pain. Is a butterfly.
That just wants to be free.

Your pain's time with you is a chrysalis. A temporary home for transformation. But all pain eventually grows wings. Don't be afraid to set your pain free. It was never meant to stay with you, become you, cage you. It was meant to teach you. Then, like all travelers, it was meant to move on down the road. To migrate the indigo sky. Set it free. Take your pain out to the woods. Or to the water. Or up a mountain. Hold a ceremony. Light a candle. Burn sweetgrass. Thank your butterfly pain for its peculiar kindness in your life. Its masterclass. Say goodbye. Offer tears. Open the cage. Set it free. Bless your tender heart forever. Butterflies don't belong trapped in your suffering. They belong in the freedom sky. So do you, dear one. So do you.

Try not to quarrel with your intuition.
It is trying mightily to help set you free.

Your intuition has saved your life more times than you will ever know. Show it some Love. Learn to notice it. Learn to trust it. Using it is how you give thanks for it. Your intuition is an always-working operating system, anti-virus program, and liberation device. It speaks in the voice of Spirit and ancestors. Many use it as a background system. You can move it to the foreground of your life. It keeps you and yours safe from harm and draws you and yours to what you need. Because it often runs silently and is invisible, you may believe it does not exist. But in every moment of your life you are flowing with your intuition's current or against it. This is how your life has ease, peace, and clarity, or difficulty and confusion. You may not even be aware of its best work, but know that it is absolutely keeping you free. Dear soul, your intuition is working tirelessly and entirely for you and your collective. Give yourself permission to live entirely in your intuition. This is how you show it Love.

You are not what hurt you. You are not the hurt. You are an entire universe. Remember that. Remember peace. Your hope and power live in your idea of you. When you feel small and overwhelmed, remember, you are infinite and able. Breathe. Remember peace.

Identify your true medicine. Hold it close.
Drink its blessings often. Permit healing.

How to heal generational trauma: Identify all the ways you have been hurt by your family, community, and society. Dig down deep and find the roots of that harm. Identify those roots in you. Spend the rest of your life patiently dissolving those roots with Love for yourself and your generations. Kiss what rises from your ground. If what rises is harmful, it will melt away. If what rises is healthful, you will have a new flower for the garden of your life.

The splinter in your soul is slavery.
The pain it causes is how freedom speaks.

Freedom from suffering requires suffering the birth pains of freedom. Be willing to do the work. Unattended suffering is endless. Freedom's birth pains come and go. What we seek with freedom is the same as what water and sugar do for each other. Water sets sugar free. Sugar sweetens water. This is how your soul and freedom can be.

After a lifetime of burden, she realized true freedom can only grow from the soul. She planted there, built her life.

Where you put down roots matters, dear one. The only true soil for an abundant life is the soul. Turn that earth and reap your harvest. When you feel yourself chasing worldly distractions, take a deep breath and call yourself home. To your soul. All your resolutions grow there. Here's to peace of the soul, for you and all living things. *All your relations.*

Self-Love is not a light switch you flip.
It is a garden you grow.
Patience, dear one.

Patience will bring you the most phenomenal flowers. Self-Love is revolutionary. It is medicine against all harmful spirit in the world. Your people need you to Love (nurture) you, so you can stand for your people. Small daily offerings to your soul become a mountain of strength and endurance over time. Allow your growth to be gradual, not spectacular. Grain by grain you make your mountain.

The most amazing thing happened as she practiced patience.
Her whole life filled with flow and peace.

The seed must have thought it would take forever to sprout. The sprout must have thought it would take forever to break through the soil. The stalk must have wondered if it would ever become a tree. The tree must have ached to finally grow into an abundant forest. You too are on your way to miracles and wonder. Patience can make hardship softer and invite ease into your life. Patience seduces your dreams, dissolves anxiety, and awakens your gifted inspiration. The creator in you grows wide-open and relaxed. Patience doesn't slow you down. It tunes you up. Dilates your soul vessels for sacred flow. Patience is self-Love, too. Practice patience, dear soul. And believe. Your abundant forest is already breaking through.

A man sat silently for days in a field of golden grass. His gaze moved from earth to grass to sky and back. His face glimmered in tears. A friend came to check on him.

What are you doing here?

I wish to finally truly experience Creation while I still breathe and live. I need to feel it in me, me in it. I have been needlessly homeless all my life. I yearn for union.

You have been here for so long. How long do you need?

Eternity.

You have so much Love in you. You want to feed your people. You give and give, emptying your vessel. Care for yourself deeply. Let your wellness be your ultimate offering. This is how you feed your people. Prepare a table filled with your abundance. Invite your people. Say, *Eat plenty*. Then, dear soul, go back to your garden and keep growing your abundance. Stay in your sacred garden. This personal soil (soul) work is the calling of your life. All the feasting comes not from your giving but from your growing. A farmer spends her life in her fields, growing, not in the market, offering. If she stayed in the market, she would have nothing to offer. Take wonderful time for yourself, guilt free and joyful. Rest, play, raise, relax, release, romance your heavenly soul.

Sacred One, spend your life being you, not explaining you. We need the light of your truth even as we do not fully comprehend it. You need the peace of being secure in your truth. So it may be fulfilled. It is good in you.

Some people will choose to spend their whole lives wallowing in self-pity, regret, blame, resentment, or negativity. They will invite you to join them in the tar pit, the quicksand of their choice. Love them from your solid, stable ground. Your circumstances don't determine your life. They fertilize your life. You determine your life. You can be all things. Determine it so.

Human culture is increasingly dehumanizing. Our work together in our time on earth is to *rehumanize*. Too many of us, including our young ones, move through life believing we are slaves to our circumstances. We mourn and grieve our experiences and conditions, wearing them like heavy shackles. This suits your oppressors, the true beneficiaries of your lack of belief in your possibilities. BeLoved, if you have been harmed, you are in possession of great healing power. A seed of potential. You can do with your life what your body does daily: repair, renew, grow stronger. What are the essential ingredients of your childhood and life circumstances? What savory recipe do you choose for these ingredients? You can make something we've never tasted before. All of life is waiting to feast.

If you feed your people your knowledge as though it is hard, stale bread, they will swallow the stone of it and suffer. If you feed your people your illumination in a warm and caring way, they will eat of it and be fed. They will become that morning glow.

What others need most from you is your heart, spirit, instinct, intuition, and caring. Not your academic, intellectual professionalism that too often is soulless, deriving from a soulless cultural mentality. Grow faith that you were born with the giftedness intended for your calling. No longer consider your life artifacts baggage. Call them your credentials. You need no artificial credentials to nurture and guide others. You were born qualified. Go ahead. Bless your people.

You have the sacred right to live intuitively.
You sense things. Use that power.

Do not be ashamed that you feel things. You have the right to feel in every space of your life. Feeling is not a weakness. Unfeeling people with unfeeling ways have conditioned you to exist only in your intellect. This is because they are terrified of the profound power of your heart and soul. They know that if you inhabit these aspects, you and your kind will be free. We make choices that cause suffering not because our intuition is bad, but because we do not believe in or use our intuition. Give yourself permission to bring all the wonder that you are to all the spaces of your life. When you were a child, you lived according to how things felt to you, like most living things. Then society shut down this part of you, told you only thinking was valid, and only thinking that affirmed the status quo. You became a good test taker, but no one showed you how to be a soul maker. Follow your intuition to water, not the crowd to thirst. Fill your spaces with soulfulness. It will soothe your tenderness. And you will have new life. Liberation is an act of bringing your whole self wherever you go.

Serenity is not your enemy, dear soul.
Give yourself to it. It will heal you.

As you puzzle peace, you no longer live as a puzzle piece. Bring all of you to all the spaces calling you. Mystic in your majesty, now you are the puzzle and the peace for those who puzzle peace.

You are alive today.
Celebrate that.

Appreciation, affirmation, and celebration are how you keep your soul supple with gratitude. Celebrate not only the grand. Celebrate the smallest grains of blessing. For they are not small at all. They are infinity in a seed. Be devoted to finding reasons to celebrate. It will change your atmosphere to Grace.

What will you do with the loneliness that comes with this calling? If you run from it, it will stalk you down. It is faster. Cook for it. It is a hungry spirit. Feed it something you Love. Feed it the ways of your people. Feed it your memories of togetherness. Even if those memories are ancestral, before your dawn. If you talk story to the loneliness, it will curl up like a small child and fall asleep to your tale. Then you can put it to bed and return to your grown folk things.

Revolutionaries should cry often, in some way. So many rivers flow into you. Many rivers should flow out. This is your equilibrium technique. You need not worry about your alkaline-acidic balance. Tend to the way you balance intake and release. Calm and duress. Hope and discouragement. Joy and sternness. Garden your harmony of things. Rivers are proud of their cleansing nature. Let the rivers in you do what they were born to do.

Easy now. You are new to this moment.

We often seek substances that alter our state of consciousness to escape our pain. But the last thing we are willing to alter is the state of our enslavement. What is the substance for altering that? Go searching.

There will be pain, you precious soul. With it, you will make your beautiful life. Take your clay of hurt in your precious hands and Love it all the way to life. Your healing will be hard. But it will never be as hard as the pain you have already endured.

Maybe your soul is a minefield of deep wounds others must navigate to be in your life. If this is so, do not beat yourself for it. Do not run around setting off explosions to lament your explosiveness. Go to each mine and kneel. Forgive yourself. Water the mines with your tears. Soften the soil. Gently remove the mines. Be patient. This will take time. No matter how hard this healing is, it is worth it. Your children and others should not have to lose their limbs to Love you.

You should not have to lose your life to the Love that is your painful tenderness.

Does your womb bleed in ways you feel are heavy, excessive, irregular? Maybe your womb is a river singing something about your soul. Something compassionate and quailing. Maybe your womb is empathic and grieving, crying a hopeful blood for all the wombs that have ever *wombed*. Your womb is your blessed indicator, truth teller. Sit by your river and Love it. Listen, in Love, to the song it sings. As its song and you grow together, your life will change into a purer water. And your womb river might just find a gentler flow of peace.

Maybe you were raised by harshness. This does not convict you to a life of being harsh. Your soul is not concrete. It is a cloud. Your heart will always pray for the soft cotton of things. Spend the rest of your life learning to be soft and gentle with yourself. That you may be so with the world. Do not believe this will make you weak and vulnerable. You will be the power of fluidity and grace, of womb and wonder. You will teach all who encounter you that a new way is possible, and a new world is here, and the hard, bruising ways of the past are an obsolete species that cannot survive our nascent climate of water and sky. Upon us is an era of intimate weavers and doulas of beautiful things. Forgive yourself. Be soft moss. Dance naked in fire light. Bellow the moon. This is your time to be alive and spilling your heart over meadows and souls. Shed the harshness that never was yours. The old world is a dying flicker. The new one has come. You have a gentle breeze nature. Let it taste the yearning sun.

The first revolution is to rest. The second revolution is to call upon your inspiring Spirit and ancestors. The third is to reckon with your identity and ideas. Fourth, touch your wounds. Fifth, roar out your pain. Cry. Laugh. Destroy your composure. Fall into a ceremony of surrender and entropy.

Once you have dissolved, dissolve the order of your revolution steps. Keep stepping. Move in circles. Gather your people. Talk your stories. Create. Create. Create. Help each other let go of attachments. Hold each other up when fear comes for you. Endure many deaths. Rejoice many births. Stay in the soil, planting. Harvest in season. Feast often. Passionately. Hold at your center the children, the oracles (elders), the eternals (ancestors). Hold Love.

When you caress a living thing, it heals and grows.
Your heart. A Lover. The world.

The world is not suddenly changing. It has always been changing. Its only nature is change. The appearance of consistency grants feelings of security. Many are privileged with this illusion of permanency. Eventually comes a moment that lifts the veil. This is that moment. Now is a season to breathe deeply into this opportunity to see life as it is: continuous transformation. Breathing is valuable when moving through change. Breathing is a release valve for anxiety, a multidirectional passage for peace. May we hold one another in beautiful breathing, according to our own capacity. May we hold each other in the priceless energy of caring. May we feed our docile inclinations for kindness, along inward and outward planes. Notice how the sun still rises, the sky still stretches. Earth yet beds our personal and collective being. All that is good in you is good in you beyond condition. All that you hope for is already here. You may not recognize it, for gifts often wear clothes we do not anticipate. They do not hew to trend or style. Today, may you set your eyes toward these modest blessings. May you look past their sometimes dreary, threatening outer wardrobe and see the naked glory they bring to living things. We say, Peace be with you. Grace be with you. All the Love and language of life, sweet life, be with you. This is not a prayer. This is testimony of Truth. These gifts *be* with you.

It is time for each of us to determine what medicine we have to offer the world. Concerned only for yourself, you fall into despair. Concerned only for your people, you fall into delusion. But when you offer who you are, what you have, to the world, you rise into purpose fulfilled. You rise into unconditional peace. What are your sacred medicines? Surely you overflow with the nectar of your own particular Grace. Find that, and give it. In your giving you lose your fear, anxiety, confusion, loneliness. Give your goodness. You shall be revealed. You shall be healed.

We wake this day, and kneel and pray. We lift our souls to Glory and say to you, dear one here on earth, Thank you. For your revolutionary soul. For you who have been kind, thank you. For you who have been unkind, thank you. For you who drink the soul water we pour, thank you. For you who forgive our imperfection, thank you. For you who honor our freedom and do not impose, thank you. For you who Love us, truly, without agenda, thank you. For you who are working in your own soul for our freedom, thank you. For you who hold on through your long season of terror, thank you. For you who choose to fill the world with Love's many flowers, thank you. For you who make medicine with your soul, thank you. For you in your fear and anxiety, in your courage and faith, in your next deep breath, in your seeing of beauty today, thank you. For trembling, thank you. For your tender places, thank you. Thank you for making this world worth living in. Thank you for what you bring to the fire. Thank you for your singular ways. For your rivers of tears. Thank you for interrupting the broadcast of hate with your soliloquy of caring. Thank you for braiding our memories with stories of you. Thank you for removing your clothes. Your awful self-ideas of self-harm stitched by generations of trauma. Thank you for roaming naked among us in your soul's true, gossamer physique. We Love you. We are Love finding you, like breeze through boulders, cherishing the beautiful being you are. You have always been our divine gift.

Freedom.

If this book touched you, you can touch it back.

Please consider writing an **online reader review** at Amazon, Barnes & Noble, or Goodreads. Reviews are a valuable way to support the life of a book and especially an independent author.

Freely **post social media photos** of you or others with the book, just the book itself, or passages from the book. Please kindly include the hashtag **#jaiyajohn.**

I deeply cherish your support of my books and our Soul Water Rising rehumanizing mission around the world.

BOOK ANGEL PROJECT

Your book purchases support our global *Book Angel Project,* which provides scholarships and book donations for vulnerable youth, and places gift copies of my inspirational books throughout communities worldwide, to be discovered by the souls who need them. The books are left in places where hearts are tender: hospitals, nursing homes, prisons, wellness centers, group homes, mental health clinics, and other community spaces.

If you are fortunate to discover one of our *Book Angel* gift books, please kindly post a photo of you with the book on Instagram, using the hashtag **#jaiyajohn,** or email it to us at **books@soulwater.org.** Thank you!

I Will Read for You:
The Voice and Writings of Jaiya John

A podcast. Voice medicine to soothe your soul, from poet, author, and spoken word artist Dr. Jaiya John. Bedtime bliss. Morning meditation. Daytime peace. Comfort. Calm. Soul food. Come, gather around the fire. Let me read for you. **Spotify. Apple. Wherever podcasts roam.**

Dr. Jaiya John shares freedom work and healing messages with audiences worldwide. He was born and raised in New Mexico, is a former professor of social psychology at Howard University, and has lived in various locations, including Kathmandu, Nepal. Jaiya is the author of numerous books, and the founder of Soul Water Rising, a global rehumanizing mission supporting the healing and wholeness of vulnerable populations.

Jacqueline V. Carter and Kent W. Mortensen served graciously, faithfully, and skillfully as editors for *Freedom*. I am forever grateful for their Love labor.

Secure a Jaiya John keynote or talk:

jaiyajohn.com/speaking

OTHER BOOKS BY JAIYA JOHN

Jaiya John titles are available online where books are sold. To learn more about this and other books by Jaiya, to order **discounted bulk quantities**, and to learn about Soul Water Rising's global freedom work, please visit us at:

jaiyajohn.com

books@soulwater.org

@jaiyajohn (IG FB TW YT)

Lightning Source UK Ltd.
Milton Keynes UK
UKHW010708120720
366376UK00001B/345